THE NORTHERN LEA
(No. 1.)

William Orr

BY

FRANCIS JOSEPH BIGGER.

Theirs it is to inherit
Fame of a finer grace
In the self-renewing spirit
And the untameable heart.
Ever defeated, yet undefeated
Of thy remembering race;
For their names are treasured apart,
And their memories green and sweet
On every hillside and every mart,
In every cabin, in every street
Of a land, where to fail is more than to triumph,
    And victory less than defeat.—S. G.

Facsimile Reprint 1998

Foreword

The most celebrated trial of the 1790s was that of William Orr, a prosperous young farmer from County Antrim, held at Carrickfergus Courthouse on 18 September 1797. After the scare caused by Bantry Bay, an increasingly frustrated government stage-managed a theatre of terror in 1797, ranging from the dragooning of Ulster to the Blaris Moor executions of four Monaghan militia men, who had sworn the United Irish oath, to the execution of Orr. Briefed by Lord Castlereagh, the government had decided that an example must be made of a leading Presbyterian United Irishman. The opportunity was provided by the trial of William Orr of Farranshane, a Presbyterian, Volunteer, freemason, *Northern Star* contributor and United Irishman. He was accused of administering the oath of the United Irishmen to two soldiers. In a dramatic atmosphere, Orr was capitally convicted on disreputable evidence by a pressurised jury. Allegations of drunken jurymen and intense manipulation circulated immediately, and Presbyterian Ulster was scandalised by what seemed to be a flagrant miscarriage of justice.

Despite a massive clemency campaign, Dublin Castle was flint-hearted. The tough-minded Castlereagh steeled his more squeamish Dublin Castle associates to carry through with the execution; the Chief Secretary Thomas Pelham observed drily: 'the question seems to be reduced to one of mere policy.' On 14 October 1797, Orr was taken from the gaol to Gallows Green where he behaved with a serenity which deeply impressed all who witnessed it. Accompanied by his fellow United Irishman Rev. William Staveley, Orr prayed, sang the 23rd psalm, and calmly recited the concluding verses of Corinthians 15:15;

> O death where is thy sting?
> O grave where is thy victory?

Before mounting the scaffold, he proffered his hat to Davy McQuillan, a Catholic cottier, in a gesture pregnant with United Irish symbolism (the McQuillans had been the leading Gaelic family in north Antrim). With the hanging rope draped around his neck, he turned to the small crowd (most had stayed away in utter abhorrence) and proclaimed in words which seared the consciousness of Presbyterian east Ulster: 'I am no traitor. I die a persecuted man for a persecuted country. Great Jehovah, receive my soul. I die in the true faith of a Presbyterian.'

Orr's execution and his exemplary conduct galvanised Presbyterian east Ulster. He was waked in Ballynure Meeting House prior to a massive Masonic funeral to Templepatrick, the most intensely Presbyterian area in Ireland. Orr was immediately elevated into a Presbyterian martyr. His 'Dying Declaration', printed in advance and distributed at his execution, declared:

'If I have loved my country, to have known its wrongs, to have felt the injuries of the persecuted Catholics and to have united with them and all other religious persuasions in the most orderly and sanguinary means of procuring redress – if these be felonies, I am a felon, but not otherwise.'

William Sampson, part of his legal team supplied by the United Irishmen, immediately issued a damning account of the trial – as part of the United Irishmen's policy of politicising the issue of law and order. They used the increasingly coercive legislation of the late 1790s to put the law itself on trial, by extensively printing and circulating their trial speeches, and theatricialising the whole process. John Philpott Curran, William Sampson, and Thomas Addis Emmett were competent lawyers and flamboyant orators. This strategy was highly successful in undermining the validity of coercive laws, in encouraging juries not to convict United Irishmen, and in deepening popular contempt for Dublin Castle and its legal policies.

Orr's judicial murder inflamed the situation. Toasts, memorial cards, rings, rosettes, tokens and ballads perpetuated his memory, and the tone of the moment was well-captured by William Drennan in his 'The Wake of William Orr.' The seething maelstrom of anger crystallised around the resonant mantra 'Remember Orr' – a rallying cry for the United Irishmen in the campaign to come. Designed to cow Presbyterian east Ulster, Orr's execution succeeded only in further inflaming it. It also sealed Castlereagh's absolute repudiation of his Presbyterian heritage, and made him the most hated man in his native Ulster.

Orr's reputation survived into the nineteenth century. The ballad 'By Memory Inspired', recalls him.

> In October ninety-seven
> May his soul find rest in heaven
> William Orr to execution was led on
> The jury, drunk, agreed
> That Irish was his creed
> For perjury and threats drove them on, boys on
> Here's the memory of the martyr that is gone

Even in the late 1890s and 1910s, the folklore surrounding his execution still survived strongly in the Presbyterian community of Antrim. Francis Joseph Bigger, who produced his *Remember Orr* in 1906, was able to draw on it. Bigger was a remarkable larger than life figure. A very successful Presbyterian lawyer, he was also a leading figure in the Gaelic Revival. He had the money and the energy to indulge his passion and his house, Ardrigh, became a notable centre of Irish culture. Bigger underwrote and edited the second incarnation of the *Ulster Journal of Archaeology*; he was a vigorous if undiscriminating collector of artefacts and memorabilia; a keen amateur archaeologist, his sheer enthusiasm led him to the discovery of many sites. He also promoted traditional music; he patronised practitioners, recreating the earlier system of aristocratic support.

Bigger was also interested in the United Irishmen and the *U.J.A.* published some remarkable material on them during his stewardship of it. His interest in Orr was a natural extension, and in 1906 he produced his biographical account. This is based on a mixture of documentary material and oral sources, and in typically indefatigable style, Bigger unearthed much new information. However, he was not a careful or scholarly writer and his book bears many signs of haste, over-enthusiasm, and carelessness. Bigger's account cannot be taken entirely at face-value and all his statements need to be checked against other sources.

Despite its flaws, his book is compulsively readable, brilliantly illustrated (notably by another of his protegés, the painter John Carey) and gathers together an amazingly detailed range of information on William Orr. No scholar of the period can afford to ignore it. It is, therefore, entirely appropriate that this book is being reprinted, under the auspices of the United Irishmen Commemoration Society, in this bicentenary year of the 1798 Rebellion.

Professor Kevin Whelan
Notre Dame University, Dublin,
23 May 1998

Acknowledgements

The United Irishmen Commemoration Society is very grateful to the following for making this book possible.

Professor Kevin Whelan for suggesting it.

Mr J.N. Montgomery, Chief Librarian, Belfast City Libraries for granting us permission to copy an original and scarce volume from their Bigger Collection. Ms Linda Greenwood of the library was particularly helpful in making copies of the original book available.

Mr Bryan McCabe, Managing Director of W&G Baird Ltd, for his advice and for producing the book at such short notice. In this respect, Ms Ellen Devine of Bairds is also to be thanked.

The Cultural Diversity Group of the Community Relations Council for providing a very generous grant towards publication. We wish in particular to thank Mr Malcolm Scott and Dr Maurna Crozier of the Cultural Diversity Group.

Do cuimne m' aṫaιр ċuз зраᵈ
зan ċрuaр ᵈaṁ ⁊ ᵈo ċuιll óṁóр
uaιm, ⁊ ᵈom' ṁáṫaιр, annраċτ mo
ċроιᵈe, aτá 'na beaṫaιᵈ fór aзam,
τaιрзιm an leaᵈaр ро.

INTRODUCTION.

T HE Volunteers of '82 had united Ireland in her demand for national regeneration, forcing a weak and corrupt government to grant concessions and remove restrictions by repeated displays of armed thousands in every county. Men of all classes, clothed and armed at their own expense, drilled by officers of their own choosing, were not to be lightly trifled with. Time and again the government—stupid, bigoted, and intolerant, with an idiot king and unscrupulous ministers—hurriedly yielded to popular demands. The convulsions in France had pulsated over Europe, throbbing through sluggish Saxon blood, forcing to frenzy the more fiery Celtic temperament, until the " Rights of Man " were well nigh deified by popular acclaim.

The volunteers, protestant to a man, had removed every presbyterian grievance, and demanded catholic emancipation, with equal rights to every subject. They permitted themselves to be dissolved in 1793 as an armed force. This was the great mistake ; this was the irretrievable blunder. Had they literally stood to their guns and demanded their rights, prepared to enforce them if necessary, there would have been no " ninety-eight ; " all the horrors of internecine war would have been prevented, and the degradation of a nation never have been brought to pass.

It is hard to say when the question of the union became definitely fixed in the mind of Pitt—probably between the years 1793 and 1795—although it was mooted before then. From that time on, at all events, his every action led up to it, all his policy was directed to carry it through. His right-hand man was lord Castlereagh, and never had minister a more faithful and willing henchman. The dissolution of the volunteers increased the ranks of the united Irishmen enormously. All those who had been imbued with patriotic ardour and a desire for reform of parliament hastened into the ranks of the popular society without a thought of where the road was leading, single minded in their patriotism, trustful in their friendships, hopeful of good results. Little they knew of the satanic ingenuity of statecraft which blocked their every effort, thwarted every motive, twisted every action, and wrecked every scheme. Pitt and Castlereagh knew everything—their spies and seducers were everywhere—as much public money was spent in secret service as on the army or the navy. Sir Ralph Abercrombie, the commander-in-chief, declared the army to be only dangerous to itself—not so Castlereagh's "battalion of testimony." The patriots plotted and counter-plotted, and Castlereagh sat at his desk in Dublin castle, with his friends in every county and a double retinue in his own town of Belfast. So adroitly did he work his puppets that they even informed upon each other, not knowing their fellow-traitors. The back-door stairs to Castlereagh's sanctum were worn bare by the traffic of creatures as only such a regime could bring forth, like maggots bred by putrefaction. The corrupting power of gold was used unscrupulously and unblushingly to bring about the national downfall. The screams of the peasants flogged at the triangle, in view of the castle windows, until poor humanity could bear it no longer and death intervened, were a fitting accompaniment to Castlereagh's song of death inside the secretary's office. Castlereagh can be well described as the evil genius of Ireland. The patriots moved heaven and earth in their efforts for reform — reform was all they wanted, all they asked for at first, and it was denied them. Then they thought of force and sought the aid of France, and the toils of Dublin castle closed around them. To use the words of Lecky, "the deliberate appeal by the government to the sectarian spirit among the protestants, and Pelham's language of eternal proscription against the catholics, soon completed the work." To permit, aye, to foster, an insurrection that would prove futile, that would raise class against class, creed against creed, drench the nation in blood and misery, and then from the chaos of strife carry through the long-desired wish—that was policy, that was statecraft—and in the end, success, if such a word may be so used; but we can only sigh and say, "Alas! that might can vanquish right."

That Pitt and Castlereagh overstepped the mark and very nearly found themselves on several occasions out of their depth and almost swamped by the force of a tide they did not calculate can readily be admitted. If the vortex had overwhelmed them no one could have grieved at a fate they well merited. Some good man would have arisen from the turmoil, the strife would have been allayed, and the ship of state would have been guided into port and not driven upon the rocks of a century of bitterness and hatred and seething discontent. It is hard, even at the end of a century, for any Irishman to look back upon these times without feeling his blood boil at the cruelties and injustice perpetrated in his native land.

It has fallen to me, brought up in the country of the northern leaders of the insurrection of '98, related to several of them, familiar with their homes and haunts, acquainted with the scenes of their deaths, a frequent visitor to their graves, their people and my people known and connected with each other, their names household words—it has fallen to me, after the lapse of a century, to be a chronicler of their lives and actions.

I have worked steadily at my task for many years during some of the spare hours of a busy life, and now I deem the time suitable for laying my accumulated store before my fellow-Irishmen at home and abroad. I have striven to repel the cruel and unjust indignities that have been heaped upon these men who led a valiant but forlorn hope, perishing in their efforts ; men whose motives have been belied, whose characters have been blackened, whose very principles have been traduced. My sole desire has been to redeem from the obloquy and scorn that alien feeling has poured forth, and place in the niches they are well entitled to occupy, men whose every action was noble, self-sacrificing, and patriotic in the highest sense, against whom the finger of self-seeking or corruption can never be pointed. One and all sacrificed everything held most dear—wealth and happy homes, life itself for the ideal set before them, the idol of their lives, national freedom and regeneration.

They may have lived before their age, but the seed they sowed and nourished with their blood has sprung up and borne fruit a thousand-fold, and their actions will ever continue to influence the life of the people until every creed and party within the four seas of Ireland are welded into a common nation, one and indivisable.

In recent years access to government and private papers has brought to light many hidden things, and explained much that was not previously understood. Local and family traditions have thus been corrected and confirmed, and I have taken every opportunity to collect illustrations of subjects fast fading away. It is hoped that these memories will form a lasting record of the deeds of the brave men who "fell and passed away," and at the same time assist in keeping their memories green in our hearts.

The men that fought, the men that failed,
The men that struggled through the night,
Remember! ye whose eyes have hailed
Their longed-for light.—E. L.

á lá féile páoraig 1906
Apo пизh
Deil feippoe
Eipe.

WILLIAM ORR.

ILLIAM ORR was thirty-one years of age, at the time of his execution at Carrickfergus, on the 14th October, 1797. A man in the full prime and vigour of life, strong and athletic, handsome and comely to a degree, with a figure a sculptor might copy. So contemporary accounts and all tradition paint him. He was confined in Carrick jail for over twelve months without any trial, and during that time he was visited by many friends. It was proposed to have his portrait painted, and for that purpose a detailed written statement of his appearance was taken down and published in the *Press* at the time. Any artist might paint his picture from this description—in fact, the portraits herewith reproduced have been so done. The following is the account referred to—

THURSDAY, 21ST DECEMBER, 1797.

As the Irish nation feels highly interested in whatever relates to the unfortunate William Orr, I take the liberty of sending you a description of his person, noted about a fortnight before the last spring assizes. I called in to see the prisoners, accompanied by F————, a gentleman of Carrickfergus. We were told those whom we wished to see were walking in the jail yard; on going down we found about ten men walking on one side of the yard, and William Orr, arm in arm with a genteel-looking man, on the other. No sooner did William Orr see us than he left his companion and accosted us in an affable manner. The following description of that ever to be venerated martyr may be relied on. I am the more scrupulous and minute, as I understand some of the Irish artists are meditating an engraving of their countryman, than which a greater treat they could not give the public. His apparel appeared to be all new and fashionable; his shirt and stock were remarkably white, and the ruffle at his breast seemed to have been plaited with great nicety and care; his coat was blue; his waistcoat was a fancy pattern, the ground of which was buff; his breeches were black kersimere; stockings were white silk and worsted, with small stripes of blue; his shoes were tied with black tape. He wore his hair short, and well powdered, with a neat fashionable round hat, which he sometimes changed for a turkey-leather cap trimmed with rich fur, and tied with green ribbon. He was precisely six feet two inches high; nothing can be conceived more completely formed than every part of his body, his foot and leg, his thigh, his shoulder, his arm and hand, were proportioned with the completest symmetry, and bespoke at once both strength and gracefulness. His step was firm, his gait bold and martial, his carriage erect, and motion alert and easy. He could neither be said to be lean nor fat—rather inclined to the latter. His chin was round and small; his mouth little; his lips thin, and his teeth as white as snow; his eyes were dark brown, neither sunk nor full, but uncommonly lively and expressive; his brow was arched and beautiful; his nose was inclined to the acquiline, though very little; his forehead was smooth, round, and well proportioned to the other features of

WILLIAM ORR

(from a painting by E. A. Morrow).

his face. In the whole countenance there was something inexpressibly captivating and manly. He possessed a sound understanding, warm affections, and a most benevolent heart.

In all the countless legions of France, and in all those who were opposed to them, since the commencement of the present war, it is a question if a finer fellow could have been found.

In describing William Orr's dress, I forgot to mention that he wore a very narrow bit of green ribbon round his stock, tied with a small knot under the chin ; his companion had the same. I observed all the prisoners to have more or less of green in some part of their dress, the greater part wore green silk handkerchiefs about their necks.

HUMANITAS.

Such was a description of the first martyr of the insurrection, written by one accustomed to careful observation, in the language of the period.

The Orrs were a strong forcible race of Scottish origin, but with none of the dourness of the southern Scot and none of their mean ways. They had not

THE ORR'S HOUSE AT KILBEG (MILL TOWN OF SHANE'S CASTLE),
WHERE WILLIAM ORR WAS REARED.

confined themselves to one spot of land, but had gone afield in their pursuit of a livelihood. It is evident from their disposition and mode of life that they had mixed blood in their veins. They were free in their opinions, political and religious, generous in their hospitality, social in their manners, sporting in their habits. William Orr was himself a member of the masonic order, belonging to a lodge in the little town of Antrim. This fraternity gave special opportunities for genial meetings, and was largely used at that period by the united Irishmen for the dissemination of their views, and frequently as a centre of republican influence and free thought. His brethren stuck closely to him in all his trials, and at the end crowded around his funeral bier, and reverently left him lying in his grave. His father, Samuel Orr, came from Coleraine to Eden-dubh-carrig (Shane's castle), where he was a purveyor to the troops lying there. His house was at Kilbeg, now called the Mill town of Shane's Castle, to the east of the little graveyard there. Here his family was born and reared. It was afterwards burned by the yeomen, but was fitted up again, and stands at the present time practically in its original state. It is a fine large roomy two-storied slated house, of a most comfortable class, with a good range of office-houses at the one side, and the remains of gardens, orchards, and plantations around it, set well back from the road. Here William and his brothers spent their boyhood before they went to Farranshane. Having made some money, Samuel Orr advanced it on mortgage to the Craigs of Farranshane, a townland

DUNEANE PARISH CHURCH,
WHERE WILLIAM ORR AND ISABELLA GREER WERE MARRIED.
(from a photo by the reverend M. Fahy, rector).

in the parish of Antrim, about a mile and a half east of the town, in the direction of Dunagore. The Craigs getting into arrears, the Orrs took over the broad acres of Farranshane, and went to reside there, erecting several houses on the land for themselves and their workpeople. It is said this action of the Orrs was much resented by the Craigs. The Orrs also started a small bleachgreen on the meadow near the little river bordering Rathbeg, the site of which is still pointed out. It was usual in the latter part of the eighteenth century for all the well to do farmers, in county Antrim, to combine some other industry with their husbandry. Therein lay much of their prosperity. Some had tanneries, others were wheelwrights, others smiths, many were bleachers, and all carried on weaving and spinning for the use of the house and often for commerce.

William Orr married Isabella, a daughter of John Greer, a bleacher near the shores of Lough Neagh, and his wife, Jane Maclelland, of Banbridge. He used to point out his wife's father's place, from his lovely home, at Farranshane, across the shimmering waters of Lough Neagh. The Greers belonged to Artlone, in the parish of Duneane, but their bleachgreen was in Tireoan. William Orr and Isabella Greer were married in 1788, by the reverend Maclusky, the curate, in the parish church of Duneane, and had six children, the last being

"The child new stirring in the womb"

when the father was executed. The parents, at their last sorrowful parting in

THE HOME OF WILLIAM ORR AT FARRANSHANE,
LOOTED AND BURNED BY THE MILITARY IN '98.
(from a restored sketch by Joseph Carey).

Carrick jail, had promised that the child when it came should be called after the father, so the heart-broken widow called it Wilhelmina, for it was a girl. The names of the other children were Samuel, Jane, John, Alice, and Isabella. Alice or Ally was also the name of William Orr's favourite sister, who died in 1796.

The home at Farranshane was a well-plenished and commodious one, built of large stones, two storied with a cellar and slated, with fine cut sandstone eaves and barges. The door was near the centre, opening into the large kitchen, to the right was *the* room and off it two small bedrooms. A great fireplace filled the side of the kitchen furthest from the door with wide swinging crook and ample hearth. Off the kitchen were two other bedrooms. The stairs rose from the kitchen to several rooms above. The furnishings were plain and substantial. In front of the house were sloping gardens and orchards planted and adorned with fruit and flowers. Two Tardree granite pillars carry the entrance gate; free flowering cherries and blackthorns were abundant; in spring-time the lane leading from the house across the fields to Antrim was carpeted with their petals.

These houses at Farranshane were much better built and planned than those

HARP HALL, FARRANSHANE, THE RESIDENCE OF SAMUEL ORR,
BROTHER OF WILLIAM ORR.
(from a photo partly restored.)

in the surrounding district. They had fine roomy cellars, clearly indicating accommodation for mercantile pursuits, and the outhouses still bear evidence that they were not erected solely for farming purposes. Bleaching and other industries must have been carried on to a considerable extent. Harp hall, as Samuel Orr's house was called, at Farranshane, was remarkably well built with cut black stone. Against the gable still remains a curious circular watch-house, overlooking the orchards and lands. It, too, was burned and sacked by the yeomen, and the charred beams can yet be seen, grim reminders of a wickedness and cruelty incredible in modern times. An old Irish yew still stands, like a death sentinel, close beside the desecrated home where once peace and plenty reigned supreme. And then what a prospect from this treasured spot, undulated woods, ploughed uplands, and wide spreading lawns stretch down the valley to where the towers of Antrim nestle by the shore of Lough Neagh. Along its margin, embowered in foliage, lie the ruins of Shane's castle, with the old round tower nearer hand, and the great double fort of Rathinra just across the burn, whilst right across the vista Lough Neagh gleams and glistens in the sunlight, or is reddened by the glory of the sunset topping the hills of Tireoan and Tirconail. To the south, close by, rise the sloping sides of Rathmor of Magh-linne, famed in bardic tale, the royal seat of the MacUillins, princes of Dalaradia, sacked by a Bruce and plundered by the stranger. High above

THE OLD PRESBYTERIAN MEETING HOUSE IN ANTRIM
WITH WHICH THE ORRS WERE CONNECTED
(*from a sketch by F. W. Lockwood*).

all rises Dunagore, keeping sentinel and guard while races come and races go. Ancient carns and residences abound on every hand, speaking of past heroes, telling of men who had struggled and fought and passed away, of an ancient civilization that had made its mark on the world's history, and has been well nigh forgotten by those who now plough the upland slope or tend the cattle upon the hill tops.

Such were the surroundings of Willam Orr when he brought his beautiful young bride to Farranshane, where sons and daughters were born to him, and he revelled in the fulness and joy of life and the ample bounty bestowed upon his household. William Orr was a presbyterian, but his wife was probably a member of the established church, as they were married in the parish church of Duneane, and at least one of their children was so married many years after by William Mortimer, curate of Antrim. They were connected with the old congregation of Antrim, of which William Bryson was minister at the time of Orr's execution. This congregation was a unitarian one, but the clergymen who attended on William Orr in Carrick jail, evidently his own personal choice, were not of that belief. William Staveley was the covenanting minister of Knocbracen, in the county of Down, and held similar political opinions to his friend; as captain of his own corps he reviewed the Knocbracen volunteers. He too was arrested at a later date, and narrowly escaped the rope. Adam Hill was minister of Ballynure and John Savage was of Carrickfergus, both orthodox presbyterians. This may be accounted for by the unpopularity of Bryson in Antrim, and also by the fact that the divisions between the different sections of presbyterians were by no means keenly marked amongst the people.

The Orrs prospered even beyond their neighbours; they bleached linen, farmed, and bought and sold horses, and hunted with the best. Shooting was their favourite sport, William and his two brothers, James and Samuel, vieing in many a contest. The three brothers were volunteers, and subsequently became united Irishmen. William worked hard for the cause, straining every nerve in his efforts to unite the people of every creed and class in their demands for absolute political and religious equality and freedom. He was a member of the head northern committee, and a contributor to the *Northern Star*, and as such, in 1796, was informed upon to the government by his associate, that most infamous Judas of the party, Samuel Turner, of Newry, "the friend of lord Downshire." Turner had early bartered his soul for the gold lavishly poured into his pockets by chief secretary Pelham. "Don't name it," writes Turner to Pelham; "if it get out they will know whence it came, and my life will be the certain forfeit." He was ever willing "to steep the evangelists in blood," but not publicly. Orr had revealed the greatest secrets of the movement to his confrère Turner, and they speedily reached the ear of Pitt. Turner had bargained that in no case was he to prosecute openly, nor was his identity to be revealed, but that "another cool five hundred" was to be forwarded to him. In the most secret correspondence of Pitt or Pelham, Cooke or Castlereagh, Turner is always referred to as "lord Downshire's friend," "Furnis," or "Richardson," and never as Samuel Turner, LL.D., of Trinity college, Dublin, barrister-at-law, the Newry renegade, the vampire who sucked the blood of his most intimate acquaintances, who was their bosom friend and their betrayer.

From this time forward William Orr was a marked man. His popularity amongst the people, his unswerving honour and rectitude, his absolute confidence in the right prevailing, in spite of the power of a most corrupt ascendency, all weighed heavily against him in the eyes of those who had a policy to carry through, regardless of all moral obligation, and an absolute negation of every principle of honour. Of William Orr nothing could be proved that would bring him within the meshes of the law. That, the government knew and felt, so they must needs make a case, and they had ample machinery for so doing. Then, again, such would be the indignation of the people at the execution of a man like Orr that the foreseen insurrection would be forced, the people taken at a disadvantage, and the country deluged in blood, so that in the anarchy of things Castlereagh might evolve Pitt's favourite scheme of a union " when Ireland lay broken and bleeding."

The French invasion was the greatest terror the government had, but the oppressed people looked keenly forward to foreign aid. To force the insurrection before such aid arrived was therefore deemed most desirable. The fate of Orr did more to hurry the insurrection than the efforts of all the leaders. It severed the last link which bound the presbyterians of the north to agitation within the law for freedom and reform, and forced them into actions leading inevitably to insurrection against an intolerable system of misgovernment and despotism.

Contemporary history proves conclusively what Pitt's designs were, and how he brought them about. I give the rough, brutal statement contained in the letter from the bishop of Cloyne (William Bennet) to the bishop of Dromore (Thomas Percy), dated 22nd October, 1798. Bennett mentions hearing talk of a "union being in agitation," and then adds, "I am inclined to think it would be far better to delay till a peace, when England with her great forces all on foot and unemployed, might drive it down by main strength if fair means would not do."

" Ill-fated country ! torrents of blood must flow—the bravest of your sons must perish to deck the funeral pyre of national independence." The chief-justice, lord Clonmell, early knew of this design : how the government fostered the insurrection, goading the people to resistance, so that when the country was prostrate Pitt's measure might be carried. He refers to the project in his diary at the very time of Orr's arrest. Lord Clonmell told the lord lieutenant that, considering the government knew all, the movement should be stopped before blood was shed. He was coldly received, and not again summoned to the privy council. There was a letter in the possession of lord Clonmell which on his deathbed, early in 1798, he asked his nephew to destroy, so ashamed was he of the government tactics. This letter clearly showed the duplicity of the authorities, and how the insurrection might easily have been prevented, "*but they let it go on, on purpose to carry the union, and that was their design.*" The policy had to be pursued, and William Orr was one of its first victims.

A net was spread for him, and he was soon caught in its toils. Ostensibly he was arrested for administering the oath of the united Irishmen to two members of Fifeshire fencibles, Hugh Wheatley and John Lindsay, colonel Derham being their officer. I doubt very much if these two men were *bona-fide* fencibles at all. I think they were simply the hook in the trap set to catch William Orr, and that their proper calling was that of paid informers. Colonel Derham was much in evidence else- where during the insurrection, particularly in Belfast, and I feel he had knowledge of the horrid plot that was being enacted, for neither he nor any other officer vouched for the characters of either Wheatley or Lindsay at William Orr's trial, although they were present and the informers were hard pressed by the prisoner's counsel, and the crown case almost collapsed in consequence. They probably did not wish to over perjure themselves knowing the characters of Lindsay and Wheatley, who were masquerading as soldiers in pursuance of a plan previously agreed upon. It was not soft-heartedness that prevented colonel Derham giving evidence, for he was the officer who, a few months later, brutally slammed the door of his house in Castle place, Belfast, in the faces of the two girls, the grief-distraught sisters of Henry Joy MacCracken, who had only implored him for an admission order to see their brother in jail prior to his execution. He then said, "if their father and mother, sisters and brother, and all the friends they had in the world were in similar circumstances he would give no such order."

The crown solicitor, John Pollock, doubtless "managed" these two fencibles just as he "managed" others according to the secret service records of the government, now made public, for we find large sums paid to him for other noted informers. A month or two after the trial, however, we find both Wheatley and Lindsay receiving their pay direct from Dublin castle in the regular list of "the batallion of testimony." On 12th December, 1797, Wheatley gets one guinea, and Lindsay two. On 1st January, 1798, "Lindsay, of the Fifeshire fencibles," gets £20. On 20th January, Wheatley gets another guinea, and on 23rd of same month, £20, and on 5th February, 1801, £115 2s. 9d. is paid to him "in full of all demands," but on 12th March succeeding, "Whitley, by direction of Cooke," crops up again for £40 19s., which may have gone to purchase a militia outfit, for he was further rewarded on the 26th of the same month with a lieutenancy in the tenth (Edinburghshire) militia. "J. Lindsay, in full of all demands, £100," appears at date, 26th July, 1799.

These are the figures, the price of these two scoundrels, that have so far met the eye of the historian; there may be others stored in the archives of Dublin castle, but these give us the market value of these two Scotchmen, Wheatley and Lindsay, according to the government scales of '98. Samuel Macskimmin, of Carrickfergus, who was himself a yeoman, describes them as "villains," and he knew his men when he had the courage to say so. According to Maxwell, " No matter how villainous the character of the wretch, his testimony during these unhappy times was received in courts of justice."

The villainy does not end here. John Philpot Curran and William Sampson were Orr's counsel, both men above suspicion as sterling advocates, but Orr's attorney, who instructed counsel, was James MacGucken, a pious catholic of Belfast, who was "managed," as we are told in the Cornwallis papers, by John Pollock, clerk of the crown. Pollock, we are pleased to note, was himself finally impeached for malpractices and degraded. We find vast sums set down opposite the name of Pollock for himself and other "managed" parties, and especially "J. Pollock, for M'G., £60," "for M'Gucken, £100," and then again £100—also, "M'Gucken, Belfast, per post, by direction of Cooke, £50," " M'Gucken, per Marsden, £50," and so on, hundred after hundred *ad nauseam.*

The whole story is abominable ; to obtain heaven itself such means as were used to convict William Orr would be unjustifiable, but the horror of the story is not half told. Fitzpatrick thinks MacGucken only turned traitor and sold his clients after the year 1798, when his name first appears in the secret service lists. Of course this is proof positive that his feet were then firmly set on the path of the traitor—that is all—from that date he stands fully revealed.

The sheriff was the honourable Chichester Skeffington, afterwards lord Massereene. He held the lucrative government post of collector of customs for Belfast, and was a man willing to oblige the powers that be in view of past favours and of future expectancies. It was he who arranged the jury which tried Orr, and it was under his personal supervision the execution was carried out. We find a jury panel in January, 1798, returned by him, with all the jurors carefully marked as to their political opinions, with the assistance of general Barber. Those jurors who differed from the sheriff were marked in degrees — (1) "timid," (2) "disaffected," (3) "bad in every sense of the word." All the jurymen so marked had been rigidly excluded from Orr's trial. Against this flagrant piece of jury-packing John Philpot Curran protested in vain. Skeffington was a labourer worthy of his hire. One little thing he did which speaks volumes— he eventually made away with all the papers relating to this period. He lived in the large house at the corner of Donegall place and Castle street, Belfast, now built over by Anderson & MacAuley. It was through his hands the blood-money passed for the informer Newell. Here is one of the entries from the secret service account:—" 2nd Feb., 1798—*honorable* C. Skeffington, what he paid Newell, £22 15s." He promised preferment to MacConnell, a sub-officer of his, in 1794, to give evidence against the *Northern Star* for publishing the address to the Volunteers, although that address had been published on a previous date in the *News-Letter,* so active was he to appear to advantage with the Dublin castle authorities. The prosecution of the proprietors of the *Star* broke down in spite of the weighted court engaged in the prosecution ; but what the "law" failed to accomplish "martial law," or organised military rowdies, subsequently succeeded in carrying out, when the *Northern Star* office was wrecked and the type thrown into the street.

The wife of Chichester Skeffington was Harriet Jocelyn, a daughter of lord Roden, who so ruthlessly slaughtered the hundreds of unarmed peasants who had surrendered on the Curragh of Kildare, well earning for his fencibles the name of "Jocelyn's fox hunters." His courage, however, oozed away at Castlebar, his horse carrying him forty miles without drawing breath at "the races" there, when the French forces routed an army vastly their superior in numbers and equipment. It was a well-matched alliance, Skeffington-cum-Jocelyn. His brother, Henry Skeffington, was M.P. for the county and sold his vote for a promise of the lieutenant-governorship of Cork, with £300 a year in addition, and was appointed clerk of the paper office of the castle, with £7,500 for his patronage. His brother William was constable of Dublin castle. The Skeffingtons ran no risks when government favours were in question. It is hard to understand these Skeffingtons, for they posed as patriots. Was this to deceive the people, or was it to run with the hare and hunt with the hounds? Four months before the trial of Orr we find this same Skeffington presiding as sheriff at a county meeting, with Luke Teeling as secretary, when a petition was agreed upon protesting against the letting loose of "all the horrors of licentious power and military force by sending bands of mercenaries in every direction . . . to plunder houses; numbers of our fellow-subjects having been banished without even the form of a trial, or are crowded into dungeons, and this only because they have dared to unite together in the vindication of common right, in the just and legal resistance of common oppression, in the kind and brotherly consolation of common suffering." Such were "the grievances of a people who knew that their title to liberty is from God and nature, which no human law can abrogate nor authority can take away." "Our complaint is against those wicked and unprincipled ministers who, to the inseparable calamities of war, have, with the most wanton cruelty, superadded the horrors of intestine tyranny and proscription, alike regardless of the rights of Ireland and of the union and safety of the empire." . . . "The constitution has given place to the bayonet."

Such was the petition formulated in May, 1797, with Skeffington in the chair and William Orr in jail. In the September of the same year we find the same man packing a jury and executing one who did not advocate one single jot more than what was then enunciated. We find him and William Bristow visiting in jail one of these people who was, to use his own words, "put out of the protection of the peace" at the behest of "wicked and unprincipled ministers," not like the visitors to Peter in prison, to bring freedom and liberty, but to inveigle an innocent man into confessing a guilt he could not feel. This Chichester Skeffington was brother to the fiery lord Massereene who let the "cat out of the bag" regarding vicar Macartney at Antrim.

John Toler, afterwards lord Norbury, "the hanging judge," was the solicitor-general, and one of the principal advisers of the crown in such cases. His reputation is well recorded. He is said to have hanged one hundred and ninety-seven men out of one hundred and ninety-eight whom he had tried on one assize, and the one escaped because he was a yeoman and had only killed a rebel. Toler was going strong for promotion, and got it. Within twelve months he was made attorney-general, the first act in his new office being the prosecution of John and Henry Sheares on the evidence of captain Armstrong, who had wormed himself into the confidence of these brothers in their own house, at their own fireside, at the express instigation of lord Castlereagh, and with the connivance of the crown officials. The traitor MacNally, counsel for the Sheares, who was in the pay of the government, had in the very middle of the trial given away to Toler the points of defence on which he was relying. It was Toler, when solicitor-general, who said that lieutenant Hempenstall of the Wicklow militia "had done no act which was not natural to a zealous, loyal, and efficient officer." This was at a trial when Hempenstall, "the walking gallows," had himself admitted hanging a peasant over his own shoulder. As lord Norbury, Toler joked with his victims as he pronounced their death sentences; he flashed his puns at the bar and set the court in a roar, turning the place into a bear garden. From attorney-general he became lord chief-justice in time to express pious regrets and other platitudes as he sentenced Robert Emmet to his doom. He has been well described as "bully, butcher, and buffoon." In later years he became such a scandal that even his former services were not considered adequate to save him, and he was hustled from the bench to find soon afterwards an ignominious grave.

Arthur Wolfe, afterwards lord Kilwarden, was attorney-general. He had been accustomed "to think uniformly with the executive power." He was looking forward keenly to a seat on the bench—to gain it he must stick close to his marching orders. Ponsonby alluded to him as "a very worthy gentleman, but a miserable attorney-general." He was considered the adviser of most, if not all, of the severe laws then enforced which suspended the ordinary constitutional rights of the subject. In doing so he was a willing instrument in carrying out the government policy. The informer MacNally played his part so adroitly that his house was once raided by the yeomen as that of a patriot, and a silver cup stolen. It was Kilwarden gave the order for its release, so he must have known the informer's true character, and no honorable man could have known that and associated with him in any way, public or private. He gained his promotion, being made lord chief justice of the king's bench the succeeding year, on the death of lord Clonmell. When lord chancellor Clare passed to his reward in 1802 and his funeral had wended its way from Ely place to saint Peter's, amidst the execrations, the throwing of dead cats, and the ribaldry of a Dublin crowd, we find Kilwarden calling upon viceroy Hardwicke for the vacant post for services rendered to the government; his nephew in the church getting ample preferment. In the year 1794 he advised and pressed the prosecution of the proprietors of the *Northern Star*, as previously noted, a most unfair proceeding, and one clearly undertaken to harry and destroy a paper not under government influence on account of its free expression of opinion. The *Northern Star* and the *Press* were both deliberately suppressed by the authorities because they were the only papers which ventilated the outrages on the people perpetrated by the yeomen and others acting under castle approval. Kilwarden met an untimely fate, being killed in the Emmet rising in 1803.

Amongst the other prosecuting counsel of Orr was counsellor Macartney, who bore the ominous name of Arthur Chichester. He was a nephew of the vicar of Antrim, another link in the encircling chain wound around the prisoner. He was made recorder of Dundalk and counsel to the chief remembrancer of the court of exchequer office. The son of the vicar of Antrim referred to later bore the same name. Another prosecuting counsel was James Dawson, who the succeeding year was made chairman of the county Armagh sessions, receiving rapid promotion.

So much for the witnesses, the attorney, the sheriff, the crown counsel, but what of the judges? They were Barry Yelverton (baron Avonmore), chief baron of the court of exchequer, and Tankerville Chamberlaine, one of the justices of the king's bench. Of Chamberlaine we know little; he was a puisne judge in every sense of the term, a mere backer up of verdicts otherwise decided upon. Of Barry Yelverton we know more. He had been member of parliament for Carrickfergus, and looked for higher judicial positions, and acted accordingly. No law officer who acted independently or did not fall in with government policy down to its very dregs got preferment at this period. Yelverton got his promotion to the bench in 1784 for opposing the actions of the volunteers at the behest of the administration, and was made a viscount for supporting the union, although he had previously striven for legislative independence. In 1802 he pressed the viceroy for the vacant chancellorship, urging past services. The services were past indeed, and the new Pharoah knew not Joseph. Chief secretary Abbot, writing to prime minister Addington, said: "lord Avonmore is so totally negligent of propriety of manners, "and so extremely embarrassed in his private concerns that it is hardly creditable "for the kings's service for him to remain chief baron of the exchequer. His very "salary is assigned to pay his creditors, by deed enrolled in his own court."

Such was the pure fountain of justice from which was to flow the cleansing flood that was to wipe away the stains of the life and character of William Orr. Truly, it can be well said that honour, heroism, purity of motive, and self-sacrifice were only found in the dock, and so it was on that fatal 18th September, 1797, in Carrickfergus courthouse.

> Truth for ever on the scaffold, wrong for ever on the throne,—
> Yet that scaffold sways the future, and, behind the dim unknown,
> Standeth God within the shadow, keeping watch above his own.—J. R. L.

Yelverton wept as he sentenced William Orr. What was it that made such men weep? Was it the thought of their innocent childhood and a loving mother before the "exigencies of state" had damned their souls and made them the creatures they were? Was it the thought of "the might have been," as they sat there decked in their ermine and scarlet robes, whilst brave men confronted them, pouring forth their inmost souls, and calling high heaven to witness their innocence and stainless honour in the cause they had espoused. The dock courted death before dishonour, the bench——look on that picture and then on this.

"Your father is a rebel," said lord Annesley, addressing the daughter of Samuel Barber, presbyterian minister of Rathfriland, co. Down, "I will commit him to the dungeon." "If attachment to his country," said the heroic girl, "constitute a rebel, my father is one, and the dungeon, my lord, is now the seat of honour."

Judge Chamberlaine survived until 1802, when the only ripples he left on the silent pool of oblivion were a few place hunters struggling for his office, "services rendered" being their only recommendation. Yelverton died in obscurity in 1805, neglected and unmourned, with a cry upon his lips like that of his compeer, John Scott, earl of Clonmell, lord chief justice of Ireland, "I am a chief justice, and an earl, but were I to begin the world again, I would rather be a chimney sweeper than connected with the government of Ireland."

In a letter from Alexander Henry Halliday, M.D., of Belfast, to the earl of Charlemont, dated 6th October, 1797, immediately after the trial of Orr, he mentions having seen a letter from Dundalk, which stated that these judges "were much delighted with the result" of their circuit, as "they had capitally convicted twenty-seven." Not a bad "bag" for these autumnal sportsmen of their fellow-kind. How many of them were as innocent as William Orr?

William Orr was arrested on the warrant of George Macartney, vicar of Antrim, and committed to Carrickfergus jail by lord Castlereagh, on the 17th September, 1796. The information had been sworn in April, so the castle had taken five months to consider the matter, giving Castlereagh ample time to consult his minions. This was under the insurrection act passed in the same year, which made the administering of the united Irishman's oath an offence punishable by death. This act was passed to place the power of life or death in the hands of those willing to assist the government policy, and opposed to popular principles, as much as any other reason. The country was flooded with villains who were prepared to swear away the life of any one who had rendered himself obnoxious to the ruling powers, earning the liberal blood money which flowed so freely from that fountain head of all corruption, Dublin castle.

Gordon, a protestant clergyman of the time, wrote :—"In the ordinary system of espionage, which formed a leading feature in the administration of the day, no means were too vile, no intrigues too low, no teaching or deception too base for some of the highest official characters to stoop to; nor was it considered incompatible with the public duties of those officers of state to intrigue with the lowest and most abandoned of society."

Curran, the advocate, in more oratorical language, describes these informers and paid castle spies and their treatment by government as follows:—"The number of horrid miscreants who acknowledged upon their oaths that they had come from the seat of government—from the very chambers of the castle—when they had been worked upon by the fear of death and the hopes of compensation to give evidence against their fellows . . . the wretch that is buried a man lies till his heart has time to fester and dissolve and then is dug up an informer." . . . "Informers are worshipped in the temple of justice, even as the devil has been worshipped by pagans and savages; even so in this wicked country is the informer an object of judicial idolatry; even so is he soothed by the music of human groans; even so is he placated and incensed by the fumes and by the blood of human sacrifice."

In itself the united Irishman's oath was absolutely innocent, and could at the present time be conscientiously taken by any Irishman, regardless of his religious or political opinions. It ran as follows :—

"In the awful presence of God, I, A.B., do voluntarily declare that I will persevere in endeavouring to form a brotherhood of affection among Irishmen of every religious persuasion, and that I will also persevere in my endeavours to obtain an equal, full, and adequate representation of all the people of Ireland.

"I do futher declare that neither hopes, fears, rewards, or punishments shall ever induce me directly, or indirectly, to inform, or give evidence against any member, or members, of this or similar societies, for any act or expression of theirs done or made individually, or collectively, in or out of this society, in pursuance of the spirit of this obligation."

The story is told of Thomas Addis Emmet, who, in the defence of a prisoner charged with administering the oath, dilated on the perfection of the sentiments there set forth, and then to clench his argument, repeated it word for word, lifting the Evangelists lying on the table, and in open court taking the oath himself, to the astonishment of the judge and all present. The act was so dramatic and yet so sincere that it was overlooked. Nothing happened to him then for that offence, but he was a marked man.

Arthur Chichester Macartney, a son of the vicar of Antrim, with his own hands assisted at the actual arrest of William Orr at the Mill town, near Antrim, during the temporary absence of his father in England. These are his own words: "Hearing that Orr's father was dying, and that William Orr would likely be at home, he mentioned the circumstance to an officer, who accompanied him to the father's house at ten o'clock in the morning and surrounded the house with soldiers. William Orr was not to be found. At length he was discovered in an outhouse." Such was the work this hopeful son of the vicarage was engaged in during the autumn of 1796. Was he emulating the action of Castlereagh who at the very same time was arresting his young friend Teeling in Lisburn with his own hands? Why was he at home in autumn and not finishing his course at Trinity college, Dublin? He had given information to the authorities about certain goings on in the college, and at once got into bad odour with his fellow-students, whom he had informed upon. He fought three duels with those who considered themselves aggrieved, and so was refused ordination, his father having intended him for the church. He was a worthy chip of the old block, being a yeoman as well a a divinity student. During his rustication at Antrim he employed his time arresting a suspected parishioner of his parent when at home attending a dying father. For such work his own father a few years later appeals to the viceroy for a job for his son, in order that he may "be taken off the hands of government." The viceroy's sword had been taken from Camden and given to Hardwicke, so government was not relieved of the incubus, and Arthur Chichester Macartney must needs go to the wars as a real soldier. He fought through the Peninsula until peace was declared, when he received a pension, and, returning home, ordination was not refused him. His patron, lord Donegall, appointed him vicar of Belfast, a worthy successor to his kinsman, Edward May. It is a strange story, but through the same war, it may be side by side, Macartney fought with John Orr, the youthful son of his victim, who had been lured away to foreign fields to try and prevent him from even knowing or brooding at Farranshane over his father's fate.

Many years afterwards this same Arthur Chichester Macartney, divinity student, divulger of Trinity college conspiracies, duellist, yeoman, arrester of suspected persons on paternal warrants, the refused to be ordained, the man of war, and finally vicar of Belfast, refers to William Orr as "a man of very moderate abilities, athletic in his frame, active, and somewhat of a sporting character among his class." *His* class, forsooth, not the Macartney class—they sported with human game when on summer holidays; poor Orr satisfied himself with sports of the field "among his class."

The "light horse" had previously gone to Farranshane to take William Orr, surrounding Jack Gourlay's house, now a picturesque ruin, on the roadside close beside the peaceful home of old William Crawford—in which I have spent many a pleasant hour—but Orr was not there. It was in Jack Gourlay's the meetings of the united Irishmen were held, and not in William Orr's own house. They took place in the barn at the north end of the long, low, thatched cottage. Jack was a herd to the Orrs, and the house he lived in was on the lands of Farranshane. He piped the insurgents to the battle of Antrim on the 7th June, 1798, and lived for many years in the old house. He it was who told William Crawford many things when a lad, and he in turn told them to me, and I have tried to faithfully set them down in this narrative. Jack Gourlay is buried in Dunagore churchyard, on the height looking down upon his old residence, where so many distressing sights had been viewed by him.

Jack's son subsequently kept the inn at Hungry hall, not far from his father's old house, on the same roadside, but nearer Antrim town. In one end of the inn William Orr's posthumous daughter, Wilhelmina, long resided, and there she died.

JACK GOURLAY'S HOUSE AT FARRANSHANE
WILLIAM ORR WAS BETRAYED BY WHEATLEY AND LINDSAY
IN THE BARN TO THE LEFT OF PICTURE.
(*restored from a photo*).

The "light horse," not finding their victim at Jack Gourlay's, passed along the old road—it was only a path then—to William Orr's own house, but he was not there. Subsequently he was taken, with the assistance of young Macartney, at the home of his boyhood at the Mill town, near Shane's castle, where he with his brothers were tending their dying father. There is a curious tradition that there were twenty-two light horsemen engaged in this foray, and that every one of them subsequently bit the dust at the battle of Antrim.

The true facts of the "swearing in" are these: A meeting of united men was being held in Jack Gourlay's barn, in April, 1796, with William Orr presiding. Jack was present, and he told the story to my informant, who knew nothing of the official documents and government details that I now record. There were also present Dick Roy, Andy Parker, David MacQuillin, David Campbell, and others. Hugh Wheatley and John Lindsay were introduced as sympathisers, by whom we are not told, for what purpose we are now fully aware. They were dressed as fencibles, and had previously been put on the trail of their victim in a public-house in Antrim. Dick Roy doubted them, and concealed himself behind some straw. After the informers had left, he said, "Boys, we are sold ; those men are spies." Wheatley, seeing they were mistrusted, threw off his side arms, saying, "If you doubt us, take them (the arms), and do what you like with us." They were not sworn, according to Jack Gourlay, but James Hope says a man named William MacIvor swore them, but all agree that William Orr did not do so, and we have his own dying declaration that he did not, so there is not the slightest reason to doubt it.

THE OLD INN AT HUNGRY HALL
WHERE WILHELMINA ORR LIVED AND DIED.
(restored from a photo).

The two Fife fencibles forthwith wended their way to the local magistrate, who was also the vicar of Antrim, George Macartney, and he promptly took their declarations and forwarded same to Dublin castle. During all this period, when we come across clergymen who were also magistrates or yeomen they appear in a specially unfavourable light; whether it is that we expect more from them than from the laity, or get less, it is hard to say. We have John Cleland, of Newtownards; Philip Johnson, of Derriaghy; James Burrowes, of Dromore, and many others all doing things with an eye to preferment that no Christian minister would now dare to be found engaged in. The reverend George Macartney, LL.D., was vicar of Antrim and Templepatrick; he also held the livings of Duneane and Cranfield, also of Skerry and Rathcavan, was a justice of the peace for the county of Antrim and a yeoman captain, so he at least might have been satisfied with his offices. Macartney had a keen business mind, if we may so judge by a trifling entry which turns up in the secret service payments of Dublin castle. "Dr. Macartney, of Antrim, for candles and firing for a guard in 1796, £1 13s. od." I take it these are the expenses incurred at Orr's arrest. Quite right vicar, "candles and firing" for state prisoners should be paid for, but not out of vicarial tithes. We would fain believe that George Macartney was trapped into this business, or did it in discharge of his ordinary duty as a magistrate, for later on it will appear that in a penitent moment he took some part in preventing the unjust sentence being carried out, yet we find in a memoir supplied by his own son, Arthur Chichester, that at the interview he had with the viceroy, in the presence of one of the judges, the judge appealed to him thus: "Mr. Macartney, if you can lay your hand on your heart and say that you don't think the evidence is sufficient to convict the man, I will recommend his excellency to respite him." Macartney refused to do so. Madden speaks well of Macartney from an interview he had with him, but documents have since come forth that were unknown to Madden, which paint the vicar of Antrim in a different colour. The following letter was written by Macartney to the viceroy Hardwicke, desiring to be taken "off the hands of government:—

"I heard yesterday, from Mr. Macnaghten at lord O'Neill's, that my old class-fellow, dean Dobbs, died on Thursday last. He was dean of Connor, a preferment worth £400, which he communicated to me, having some thoughts of exchanging with me for some of my preferments for his sons, if it could be accomplished. My son, who was recommended to your excellency, by lord Pelham, on the ground of public services, and who is at present a first lieutenant in the artillery, has taken his degree in Dublin college, and has attended the course of Divinity lectures, by which he is qualified to be ordained. May I, on the ground of both our services, suggest to your excellency the measure of appointing me to the deanery of Connor, in which diocese I have been a beneficed clergyman for upwards of thirty years, and leaving me to apply to the marquis of Donegall, from whom I got all my preferment in the church as a private patron, in order to get my son presented to some of my parishes; by which means my son and I would be taken off the hands of government; and I trust your excellency will be of opinion that my request is not unreasonable.

"In case this request cannot be at present complied with, I trust you will not take this application amiss.

"I am your excellency's most obedient, humble servant,

GEO. MACARTNEY."

The viceroy had too many such like applications, so Macartney met with a cool rebuff, which may have been induced by the following letters which he received from lord Massereene:—

"I have cautioned you against Macartney. You actually, my lord, gave a corps to "Macartney, the vicar of Antrim, of which he now, to the no small amusement of the public, is

"positively captain. He now appears in the quadruple capacity of doctor of laws, vicar of the
"church, justice of the peace, and *military captain.* Cerberus had but three heads, but Macartney
"has four. The country is on the titter, and in faith well they may, my lord."

Lord Massereene then took it into his head to put on some of his own corps to guard the town, although they had not yet been put on permanent duty. This Macartney resented, and the scene is thus described by Massereene :—

"This morning a company of blackguards and wretches, below all description, were
"assembled in the market house by Macartney, the vicar of this place, . . . they are rebels
"almost to a man. Such a tumultuous bloodthirsty rabble, I will be bold to say, you never saw,
"my lord, nor did Europe, but in France and Ireland. . . . Macartney in the distortion of a
"paroxysm of rage, foaming at the mouth like a man in a canine madness, after the most insane
"and wild, frantic declamation, declared he would have me broke of my commission. . . . Oh,
"my lord, is it possible that government would ever confide a military department to this atrocious
"villain, a man than whom a more mad exists not out of Bedlam, a coward who ran away from
"Antrim when the battle commenced. . . . For God's sake, my lord, no innovation, and
"above all things no infernal monster like Macartney, the vicar not of Jesus Christ, but of Satan."

Massereene may have been mad, but there was some truth, all e same, in his blunt statements. It was hard to please all parties, and so George Macartney found it. Too hard it was for him to place his hand upon his heart and say William Orr was perjured against, a fact which he must have known and believed, when he wished to stand high with an iniquitous government that was doling out deaneries worth £400 per annum and such trifles, for services rendered by its "most obedient humble servant."

I find another reference in the Hardwicke MSS. to Macartney, which contains a double sting. First, in reference to the vicar's flight when personal danger was involved, and, secondly, to his treatment of Orr, so both questions must have been discussed at the time. It runs as follows :—

"Antrim, 27 July, 1803.

"Macartney, the vicar of this parish, the same who ran away from the battle of Antrim, and did not return to Antrim for a fortnight, the famous Macartney who solicited both *for* and *against* William Orr, who was executed."

I have a copy of an extremely rare pamphlet published in 1797, which I largely transcribe, with some necessary corrections, as it gives the best account of the trial of William Orr, and is very little known, and quite inaccessible to ordinary readers. Its scarcity is explained by the fact that every copy that could be obtained was destroyed by the military, and any one known to possess a copy was liable to summary execution. The writer of it was William Sampson, one of William Orr's counsel, who was familiar with all the facts. I have made some additions and alterations, and added several extracts from the *Press*, to make the whole as complete as possible, and at the same time save repetition. I have not interfered with the sense or purport in any way.

Photo by W. Swanston.

VIEW OF THE RERE OF "HIS MAJESTY'S JAIL FOR THE SAID COUNTY AT CARRICKFERGUS," WHERE WILLIAM ORR WAS IMPRISONED.

COUNTY OF ANTRIM,   By the honourable Robert Stewart, commonly called lord viscount
       TO WIT.   Castlereagh, one of his majesty's justices of the peace for said
                    county.

To the high and petty constables for said county, and their assistants, and to the keeper of his majesty's gaol for said county at Carrickfergus.

I hereby send you the body of William Orr, who stands charged by examination on oath, TAKEN BEFORE THE REVEREND GEORGE MACARTNEY, one of his Majesty's justices of the peace for said county, with HIGH TREASON, which examinations upon oath have been laid before me.

These are therefore in his majesty's name, &c., &c.

                      Signed,   CASTLEREAGH.

At the Lent assizes, 1797, William Orr was arraigned on an indictment framed under the insurrection act for administering unlawful oaths. He then pleaded not guilty, but his trial was postponed on his affidavit stating the absence of a material witness.

At the late assizes he was put upon his trial on Monday, the 18th day of September, before lord chief baron Yelverton. Two witnesses appeared against him, one of the name of Hugh Wheatley and another of the name of John Lindsay, both private soldiers in the Fifeshire regiment of fencibles.

COUNSEL FOR THE CROWN.

Att. general, Arthur Wolfe (afterwards lord
    Kilwarden).
Arthur Chichester Macartney.
Edward Mayne.
James Dawson.
William Parkinson Ruxton.
Attorney, Thomas Kemmis (crown solicitor).

COUNSEL FOR THE PRISONER.

John Philpot Curran.
William Sampson.
Attorney, James MacGucken.

Wheatley swore that in April, 1796, he had been in Scotland on furlough, and was on his return by Antrim to join his regiment, then quartered at Derry; that he then, upon the 24th or 25th of that month, met with several persons who swore him into the brotherhood of united Irishmen, and afterwards took him to the house of the prisoner, whom they found employed in sowing flax in his field. He swore that an assembly was called in the house of the prisoner, who acted as chairman or secretary, which he called a baronial committee, and that there it was debated whether he should be entrusted with the printed constitutions of the society in order to promote the institution among his fellow soldiers; that it was agreed that he should have one; that an oath was thereupon administered to him by the prisoner, which was to keep the secrets of united Irishmen, and not for any reward or punishment to discover on them. The witness threw in many circumstances about arms and a northern star, which were shewn to him, also a draw-well, to put the aristocrats into.

He swore that all he did was through fear of his life, which they threatened. That he was told they had armed men enough to get a reform by force, if they could not by fair means; and that if they did not get a reform by fair means they would overturn the government. He said that the intention of the Society, and consequently of the prisoner, was to assist the French; that it was so explained to him, and that at that meeting it was so determined; and added many circumstances of aggravation tending to represent the oath and the association as heinously wicked and treasonable.

And at same time swore that the book from which the oath was administered was given to him as his guide. On his cross-examination by John Philpot Curran, he denied that he had ever offered to desert or asked for money with that view from anybody, but was offered money to induce him by a person in Belfast, which he refused. He was asked if he had sent any cartridges to William Orr, when in prison, as a token? and answered he believed not. He was asked whether he ever told any person that he had taken the test of a soldier in a certain way that suited his own mind best, and that he never was satisfied as a soldier? This he denied, but after some pause went on, "unless it might be to some of the united Irishmen before I knew what they meant." He denied that he ever said he intended to desert, tho' he might have said he was drunk when he enlisted.

THE "DEEP DRAW WELL" AT FARRANSHANE.

Question.   Had you ever any conversation with one Walker, a soldier, about being UP?

Answer.   I never advised him to be UP.

Question.   Had you ever any such conversation with Walker?

Answer.   I might endeavour to learn what he knew about being UP.

Question.   Did you ever tell him he might take the oath of secrecy without going further?

Answer.   I told him I would show him what was in my pocket-book, which was only a parcel of old letters.

Question.   Did you ever tell him how you united men got powder from abroad in flaxseed hogsheads, and how you had smiths at work making you pikes?

Answer.   I never told him of powder; what I might have told him about pikes was only in the way of a whim.

The second witness, Lindsay, did not attempt to swear anything of the words, nor even of the nature of the oath, whether it was innocent or guilty, lawful or unlawful. He only said he was in the room when an oath was administered, and of course was dismissed by William Sampson without any cross-examination as a witness, whether swearing false or true, totally immaterial.

Here the evidence closed for the crown.

Lecky unfairly makes a point of the absence of the witnesses who were present at the alleged administering of the oath to refute Wheatley. How could it be expected of men to volunteer such evidence, thus leaving themselves open to capital conviction? William Orr would be the last to desire his friends to place themselves in such jeopardy. Not one of them was, however, forthcoming to substantiate the informer Wheatley, although the same authority states their names were revealed to government.

The counsel for the prisoner [John Philpot Curran and William Sampson] contended that the jury should be discharged of the indictment, or that they should be directed to acquit the prisoner. In support of this objection, it was said that the testimony of the informer must be supposed to be true—and if it was true, the guilt which it proved was not a crime of felony under the insurrection act, but a crime of high treason, under the statute of Edward III. To meet deliberately and resolve upon arming and joining an invading enemy in the subversion of the constitution might not perhaps be an overt-act of compassing the king's death, but it was clearly an overt-act of levying war, within the twenty-fifth of Edward III. This no lawyer could controvert; the charge was therefore a charge of high treason, for which the prisoner could not legally be tried under this form of indictment. A man charged with high treason in Great Britain has advantages of defence which makes it almost impossible for an innocent man to fall a victim to the mere malice of persecution; he must have a copy of the indictment—the overt-act must be expressly charged; the blasted breath of one venal informer cannot destroy him. In that country there must be two witnesses at the least. Even in Ireland, where life does not seem to be of so much value, the man accused of treason has advantages peculiar to his situation; he is entitled to an exact copy of his charge, and a full defence by his counsel in point of law and in fact. The state must avow itself as the prosecutor—it cannot wage a piratical war against his life under false colours; and if it prosecutes him maliciously he is authorised by his counsel to display every circumstance of his case to his jury, and of appealing to every sense of their duty, their justice, their humanity, and their danger for his protection. To try him, therefore, under this act, which gave him none of those advantages, was to try him without hearing him, and was an oppression unwarranted by the law of the land. This objection, it was said, might appear at first sight to be novel and hazardous. As to its novelty, it was the first time that such a proceeding was ever attempted, and the objection to it must be, therefore, new. It might certainly be thought desperate to seek a refuge from a charge of felony under the law of treason—and it was only to be lamented that the melancholy state of the country so fully justified such a conduct.

Lord Yelverton and judge Chamberlaine over-ruled the objection.

Charles Maclaverty was called by the prisoner, who contradicted expressly some parts of the evidence which Wheatley had given upon his cross-examination, in order thereby to impeach his credit.

John Young was also examined.

Sergeant Miller was called to refute Charles Maclaverty's reliability.

The rev. Foot Marshall, presbyterian minister of Ballyclare, was called to substantiate it.

Several officers of the Fifeshire fencibles were present in court, but none of them were called to give evidence of the character of the soldiers.

The court summed up the evidence minutely, and left the consideration of the credit due to the witnesses entirely to the jury, who retired about six in the evening to consider of their verdict.

About seven the court adjourned. The jury sat up all night.

About six in the morning the court was opened by lord Yelverton solely, and, as we are informed, the jury then required to know whether they might not find some qualified verdict, of the prisoner's having administered an unlawful oath, which should not affect the life of the prisoner.

When asked by the clerk of the crown if they were agreed, no answer was made for some time. The question being repeated, the foreman, much distressed, answered, WE LEAVE HIM IN YOUR LORDSHIP'S MERCY—HE IS IN YOUR LORDSHIP'S MERCY, on which the judge desired them to return and consider their verdict, as they must return a verdict of guilty or not guilty. Ten of them only retired, two remaining without. They returned again, and very nearly the same thing was repeated, and it was not till the third time, the foreman still hesitating to pronounce the word guilty.

James Macnaghten, one of the jury, reprimanded the foreman [Archibald Thompson], calling upon him to pronounce the prisoner guilty, upon which the foreman, who was a man in years and affected even to the loss of speech, handed in the verdict, with a recommendation to mercy, which was taken by the clerk.

Lord Yelverton told them that he would transmit their recommendation to government, but that he could promise nothing as to its success.

During the whole of the trial the silence and anxiety of a crowded audience were singularly solemn and striking. The general character of the prisoner, his numerous family, the great beauty and manliness of his person, and the quiet fortitude which he displayed, when contrasted with his accusers, seemed to excite a general interest in his favour.

The judge mentioned in court subsequently that he had not pledged himself to do so, but had immediately transmitted by express the recommendation of the jury.

On the next day William Orr was brought into court to receive sentence, and his counsel then made a motion in arrest of judgment, which he supported by a long legal argument of great erudition with his usual ability and skill.

The court declared that they did not think the objections valid, and therefore refused to arrest the judgment. Shortly after, and before William Orr was remanded, his counsel stated that a most extraordinary event had just come to their knowledge, and which they thought it their duty to apprize the court of. Two of the jurors had made an affidavit, stating that on the night of the trial a considerable quantity of spirituous liquor was conveyed into the jury-room and drunk by the jury, many of whom were greatly intoxicated, and threatened the two jurors who made the affidavit, and who admitted themselves also to have been in a state of intoxication, to prosecute them as UNITED IRISHMEN if they did not concur in a verdict of GUILTY ; and that at length, worn out by fatigue and drink, and subdued by menaces, they did, contrary to their judgment, concur in that verdict. Here the counsel were interrupted by justice Chamberlaine, who declared that such a statement ought not to be permitted ; that it was evidently calculated to throw a discredit upon the verdict, and could not be the foundation of any motion to the court. The counsel said that they did not mean to make it the ground of a motion ; that they did intend, had the court permitted it, to move that the jury should be punished for their misconduct ; that, as to discrediting the verdict, if such misconduct of the jury could discredit it, it was only justice to the public and to the prisoner that it should be discredited ; that, as to themselves, they had discharged their duty to the best of their judgment, and submitted.

Curran then produced to the court the affidavits of three respective jurors in the cause, in order to shew that a most fatal injustice would be done in pronouncing sentence of death, and that where the proceedings had been such as appeared by these affidavits, a new trial should be had, lest the verdict so obtained might disgrace the administration of the law and produce consequences the very reverse of those which were sought to be produced by public examples of this terrible and awful kind. Curran had gone the length of stating the fact of the drunkenness of the jury and the threats used by some of them, and would have stated the affidavits fully, but was interrupted by the court before he had gone through them, upon the ground of the indelicacy towards the jury. The attorney general, with some warmth, expressed his astonishment at the mention of a new trial in a capital case. The prisoner's counsel was ready to produce authorities. The attorney general said if there was any ground to attach the jury that the counsel might move upon it. Curran thereupon moved that the jury be attached, but was stopped by the court, as before mentioned, who observed that, however proper such application might be to a higher power, they could not sit to hear it now in court, and the prisoner was remanded to gaol.

AFFIDAVITS OF THE JURORS.

" Arthur Johnston and Archibald Thompson, two of the jury who were impannelled to try
" William Orr, depose, on the Holy Evangelists, and say that, after they had retired to their jury-
" room to consider their verdict, two bottles of very strong whiskey spirits were conveyed into their
" jury-room through the window thereof, and given to, and the greater part thereof drank by, the
" said jurors, some of whom became very sick and unwell, which occasioned their vomiting before
" they gave their verdict. And deponent Thompson says that he was, by age and infirmity and
" intimidation used to him by James Macnaghten, one of said jury, induced to concur in said
" verdict contrary to his opinion.

" Sworn before me this 20th day
" of Sept., 1797, in court.
" YELVERTON.

" Arthur Johnston.
" Arch. Thompson."

" George Brooks, of Inisloughlin, in the county of Antrim, farmer, maketh oath and saith
" that he, this deponent, was one of the jury who was on the trial of William Orr, who was charged
" with administering oaths. Deponent saith he was resolved to acquit the said William Orr but
" for the representations of some of his fellow-jurors, who informed this deponent that in case they,
" the said jury, should return a verdict of guilty the said William Orr would not be punished with
" death. Deponent further saith that if he had at that time known that the consequence of
" returning a verdict of guilty on the said William Orr would be punishable with death, he, this
" deponent, in that case, would not have consented to such a verdict, but would have insisted and
" persevered in returning a verdict of the said William Orr's not being guilty.

" Sworn before me this 20th day
" of Sept., 1797, in court,
" YELVERTON.

" George Brooks."

It was on the last occasion that Curran made a display of touching eloquence which has been seldom equalled. He drew an affecting picture of the situation of his client, where the mere announcing of the truth might pull down resentment upon him from that quarter where resentment would be certain death, and whilst the dagger was in his heart, the very groans which he should utter, or the blood which might issue from his wounds, might be used as a justification of the poniard. He knew the terrible reply to which he might be subjecting his client. He knew how easy it was for those who wished to crush him to set their foot upon his neck and extinguish him

AFTER THE TRIAL OF WILLIAM ORR—THE COURT HOUSE AT CARRICKFERGUS,
18TH SEPTEMBER, 1797.
(from a photo by William Swanston and drawing by Joseph W. Carey.)

and his complaints for ever. But the truth was the case upon which he was instructed to insist. The truth was the case upon which only the prisoner had chosen to commit his destiny.

When the prisoner was put to the bar to receive sentence of death, the recommendation of the jury having produced no effect, the court was crowded with spectators, in whose countenances was impressed that public feeling which his fate had occasioned. Lord Yelverton addressed him in a tone of voice so low as scarcely to be distinguishable, and on pronouncing the words, "you are

36

"to be taken to the place from whence you came, from thence to the common place of execution, "the gallows, there to be hung by the neck until you are dead," the tears burst from his eyes, his head sunk between his hands, and in that attitude he remained for nearly ten minutes, during which time the prisoner eyed him with a kind and compassionate countenance, and, as soon as he raised his head, begged leave to say a very few words, which were as follows :—

"My lord," said he, that jury has convicted me of being a felon ; my own heart tells me that "their conviction is a falsehood, and that I am not a felon ; if they have found me so improperly, "it is worse for them than for me—for I can forgive them, and am not afraid to die. I wish to "say only one word more, and that is, to declare upon this awful occasion, and in the presence "of God, that the evidence against me was grossly perjured—grossly and wickedly perjured."

Having said this, he walked from the bar with a firm and undaunted step, and was re-conducted under a strong guard to the gaol.

Through the whole of this trial not only the outside hall but the interior of the court was crowded with armed soldiers, to the exclusion of many of the freeholders ; and these soldiers were appointed to act as bailiffs, with their bayonets fixed. But deeply as the public mind was affected, no disorder, not even a murmur, was heard from any quarter, and during the whole scene the prisoner alone seemed untouched with dismay.

In the interval of public suspense, between the day of pronouncing the sentence and the Saturday, the 7th of October, appointed for the execution, various representations were made to government (it is supposed) for and against the prisoner, but one in particular, on his behalf, by the reverend George Macartney, D.D., the magistrate, as appears by the committal, who took Wheatley's examinations against him, and was principally concerned in his prosecution, who, on the circumstances detailed in the following affidavits coming to his knowledge, procured the depositions upon oath of the two reverend gentlemen therein mentioned and immediately repaired to Dublin, where he laid them, together with his own affidavit hereto subjoined, before his excellency, the lord lieutenant, and used every conscientious exertion to prevent this afflicting execution from being enforced.

The following were the jurymen :—

Archibald Thompson.	Samuel Hemphill.
George Brooks.	William Laughlin.
James Macnaghten.	George Casement.
George Pentland.	Arthur Johnston.
J—— Bell, of Prospect.	John Hall.
George Dickson.	George Patterson.

The foreman, Archibald Thompson, of Cushendall, was an aged man. His was a pitiable case. He did not wish to bring in a verdict of guilty, but was bull-dogged into it by James Macnaghten. It was a Macnaghten who gave vicar Macartney the "tip" at lord O'Neill's about the vacancy of the deanery of Connor. We also find his relative, A. E. Macnaghten, M.P. for the county, bidding for government favour at a later date, and selling his vote for the searchership of Cork, with £5,000 a year, which he did not get, through an informality. He was, however, appointed a lord of the treasury instead. He was a juryman on the *Northern Star* trial in 1796, and was objected to because he had prior to the trial expressed the opinion that the proprietors "ought to be punished." So his opinions were well known and appreciated by government. Poor old, decrepid Thompson struggled hard to do the right, but was borne down by the overwhelming odds of terror and intimidation. Mary MacCracken, in a contemporary letter, dated 27th Sept., 1797, says: "Old Archibald Thompson, of Cushendall, was foreman of the jury, and is thought will lose his senses if William Orr's sentence is carried into execution, as he appears already quite distracted at the idea of a person being condemned to die through his ignorance, as it seems he did not at all understand the business of a juryman. However, he held out from the forenoon till six o'clock in the morning of the day following, though, it is said, he was beaten and threatened with being wrecked and not left a sixpence in the world on his refusing to bring in a verdict of guilty. Neither would they let him taste of the supper and the drink which was sent to the rest, and of which they partook to such a beastly degree. It was not, therefore, much to be wondered at that an infirm old man should not have sufficient resolution to hold out against such treatment." Arthur Johnston, another juror, supported Thompson in his affidavit. The only other juror who stands out from the unholy dozen is George Brooks, and he pleaded that he was deceived, and he doubtless was. George Casement was of Larne. He never fully regained his popularity there, and had to fly the country for a time to escape assassination. The united leaders exerted every influence to prevent popular vengeance falling on these jurors, as the public mind was very much inflamed against them.

The execution was respited until Tuesday, the 10th, and from thence till Saturday, the 14th October, during which period it was confidently hoped that a pardon would follow.

Colonel Barber wrote to Dublin castle complaining about the rejoicings amongst the "disaffected" at the prospect of the respite of the sentence on William Orr, and expresses the hope that the victim will not be pardoned, as in such a case "no jury would convict" in future. This gallant officer had certainly no desire to be considered amongst the "disaffected" in any leniency to be shown to the prisoner; no one would expect it of him.

An intimation having in the meantime come to the prisoner's friends that, provided the leading gentlemen of the county would memorial in his favour, mercy would be shewn. A memorial was drawn up, with the above affidavits annexed, which was signed by many, with several reasons assigned by different memorialists for interfering on his behalf, some representing it as a matter of policy to mitigate the sentence, others speaking of it as a subject of mercy, others as a measure of justice. During this doubtful period the following publication appeared in the *Belfast News-Letter* of the 2nd October, 1797 :—

" We hear from the best and most respectable authority that William Orr, now under
" sentence of death in Carrickfergus, has given under his hand-writing an acknowledgment
" of his crime and of the justness of his sentence, which he had been induced thus publicly
" to do to ease his conscience and to acquit the jury, who had been much calumniated on
" account of the verdict they had returned against him."

Upon this the prisoner wrote the following letter, with which he despatched his brother to Dublin, and, by means of the reverend doctor Macartney, it was delivered to the lord lieutenant :—

This letter entirely repudiated the above " respectable authority," which was clearly inspired by castle influence, and absolutely vindicated the innocence of the victim. The supporters of the ascendency were always " respectable," according to themselves; they never grew tired of parading in that guise. The word has now a double meaning in Ireland in consequence of such misuse.

One of the "respectable" authorities, Andrew MacNevin, according to Lecky, wrote to the viceroy from Carrickfergus that " mr. Skeffington and the rev. mr. Bristow can testify on oath that the declaration or confession forwarded to his excellency was acknowledged by William Orr to be his, and that his mind was light after it." I turn up three entries concerning this "respectable" creature in the black list :—" 27 Nov., 1797—Captain A. McNevin, £150." " 22 May, 1800—Andrew McNevin, by post to Carrickfergus, £300." " 1 January, 1801—A. McNevin, Carrickfergus, per his letter, £140 10s." His other services are unrecorded as yet. Meantime, he is fit company for Wheatley and Lindsay, as he appears on the same page with them "as per affidavit of mr. Cook." So much for his disinterested "respectable" testimony.

COPY OF A LETTER WRITTEN BY WILLIAM ORR, FARMER, TO THE LORD LIEUTENANT.

MAY IT PLEASE YOUR EXCELLENCY,

Having received from your excellency's clemency that respite from death which affords me the opportunity of humbly and sincerely thanking you, I avail myself of the indulgence of pen and paper and of that goodness which you have already manifested towards me to contradict a most cruel and injurious publication which has been put into the newspapers, stating that I had confessed myself guilty of the most enormous crimes which a perjured and miserable wretch came forward to swear against me. My lord, it is not by the confession of crimes which would render me unfit for society that I expect to live ; it is upon the strength of that innocence which I will boldly maintain with my last breath, which I have already solemnly affirmed in a declaration I thought was to have been my last, and which I had directed to be published as my vindication from infamy ten times more terrible to me than death. I know, my lord, that my own unhappy situation, the anguish of a distracted wife, and the mistaken tenderness of an affectionate brother have been resorted to to procure that confession ; and I was given to understand my life would have been spared me upon such conditions. I as decidedly refused, as I should now, though your excellency's pardon were to be the reward. Judge, then, my lord, of the situation of a man to whom life was offered upon other conditions than that of a confession both false and base. And lastly, let me make one humble observation to your excellency : that the EVIDENCE should be STRONG INDEED to induce a conviction that an industrious man, enjoying both comfort and competence, who has lived all his life in one neighbourhood, whose character, as well as that of all his stock, had been free from reproach of any kind, who certainly, if allowed to say so much for himself, would not shed the blood of any human creature, who is a husband and father of a family, would engage himself with a common soldier in any system which had for its end robbery, murder, and destruction ; for such was the evidence of the unfortunate witness Wheatley. If upon these grounds and the facts already submitted to your excellency I am to be pardoned, I shall not fail to entertain the most dutiful sense of gratitude for that act of justice as well as mercy ; and, in the meantime humbly,

I beg to remain,

Your excellency's

Most obedient and humble servant,

WILLIAM ORR.

CARRICKFERGUS GAOL, 10TH OCTOBER, 1797.

It was about this time that the prisoner's wife wrote a letter to lady Camden, of which the rough draft has accidently fallen into the reporter's hands, which as far and as nearly as it can be made out, being in some few places interlined and scarcely legible, is in these words :—

TO HER EXCELLENCY THE COUNTESS OF CAMDEN.

"Grief like mine admits of no apology—despair and sorrow are my only companions, yet "hope bids me look up to you for happiness. A miserable object, a mother and a wife, comes "praying for mercy to the father of her children. Pardon, most gracious lady, the phrenzy of a "distracted woman, and listen to the petition of the miserable wife of the unfortunate William Orr. "I come a suppliant, a low and humble slave of misery, praying your ladyship's intercession on "behalf of the life of my husband, whose existence is dearer to me than my own. Oh, hear my "complaint, and grant me one beam of hope to frantic imagination. You are the only person who "has it in your power to remove never-ending misery from a wretched individual, to cheer the "afflicted heart, to give comfort and consolation to her that was ready to perish. Suffer me to "assure you that he is innocent of the crime for which he is under sentence of death. Oh, cruel "sentence, that will, without your interference, tear from me my husband and rob my five poor "little unoffending children of their father ; the best of fathers, the kindest and dearest that ever "lived. They join in solicitations for his life ; their innocent, fervent, grateful prayers will rise as "a memorial before the throne of God ; their lisping tongues shall be taught, with unceasing "gratitude, to bless and adore the noble, generous, exalted character of their benefactress, the "revered and loved countess of Camden, how will that name be imprinted on their very souls, "never to be effaced. Forgive my importunity—the life of my husband, the father of my children's "life is at stake. Despair has almost driven me mad. I call on you to exert yourself to save his "life, thy God will reward thee, thy country thank thee, his children will bless thee if thou grantest "my petition ; and when length of years and increase of honour shall make thee tired of earthly "joys, and the curtain of death gently close around thy bed, may the angels of God descend and "take care that at the last human existence shall not receive one rude blast to hasten its extinction. "At that awful period, may the recollection of your successful interference be added to the prospect "of your future felicity   .   .   .   ."

THE FOLLOWING LETTER WAS WRITTEN BY THE PRISONER TO HIS WIFE :—

" Carrickfergus, Saturday Morning [14 October, 1797].

"MY DEAR WIFE—I now think proper to mention the grounds of my present encouragement, under the apprehension of shortly appearing before my merciful God and Redeemer, my entire innocence of the crime I am charged with. Secondly, a well-founded hope of meeting a merciful God. Thirdly, a firm confidence that that God will be a husband to you and a father to your little children, whom I do recommend to His divine care and protection, who has protected me from my mother's womb. And my last request is : that you will train them up in the knowledge of that religion, which is the ground of my present comfort, and the foundation of that happiness, I trust, I shall shortly enjoy, in that day when we must all appear before the great Judge of judges and Ruler of all. Farewell, my dear wife, farewell !

"WILLIAM ORR."

WILLIAM ORR IN CARRICKFERGUS JAIL
(*from a photo by W. Swanston and drawing by Joseph Carey*).

The writer, "Humanitas," who gave in the *Press* the detailed account of the appearance of the condemned man, also wrote the following account of his interview with him :—

I asked him if he felt very unhappy under his confinement? At first, said he, it was very irksome, but time has made it more tolerable. I hope, said I, that you have no fears for the ensuing trials? None, said he, if we get justice; but we understand they are using infernal measures to fill the jury panel.

He then asked me some general questions respecting the state of the country, talked of the dreadful bondage under which the people laboured, and the melancholy prospects that were before us. Have you heard, said he, of the dreadful vow of colonel Derham, of the Fifeshire fencibles, that he would murder all the prisoners in case the French landed. I answered that I had, but did not believe it, as I could not conceive it possible that any man, however inhuman or unprincipled, could entertain such a shocking sentiment, much less put it in execution. He then assured me that it was a truth, and added that one of the prisoners had said, in the hearing of two or three soldiers, for the purpose of having it carried to the colonel, "Yes, the cowardly villains may butcher us in our cells; but, if there is a God in heaven, the Irish nation will avenge our blood, sooner or later, while there is a Scotch or an English man to be found in the land." I told him I hoped matters would terminate more amicably between government and the people than what was generally imagined. He remained silent for some seconds, shook his head, and then said he had no such expectation; government would grant the people nothing; he saw clearly their system—Ireland must suffer. Do you recollect, said he, what a certain lord uttered in a certain assembly lately? Not just now, said I. "Much blood must be spilt in the north," said he. I observed that expressions of that kind were sometimes thrown out for political purposes. No, no, said he; you may depend upon it that there is some system laid down which has for its object murder and devastation.

I asked him if they were permitted to read newspapers. He told me they were, and that he had that morning read a speech of Charles James Fox, part of which brought the tears to his eyes. He speaks as feelingly of the distresses of Ireland, said he, as if he were an Irishman.

He then asked me if I had seen a statement in the papers respecting the French being about to invade the three kingdoms. I told him I had; and, said he, in that case I doubt there will be bloody work. I wish to God, said he, that the people of Ireland could obtain their wishes without any assistance from France. I told him that it was not likely that a connexion with France would much better our condition. Connexion, said he, I would have connexion with none of them; except a connection that would secure to us independence, liberty, and commerce. O, if Ireland was wise and united, she would soon be free and happy. O, if God would give the king wisdom to change the ministry in due time, what a happy thing would it be for the country. What calamity and woe would it prevent. He said he never pitied the catholics half so much as since he was put in prison; it was no wonder they complained, for they had suffered cruelly; and now other people were suffering as much as them, and it soon would be quite an universal complaint through all Ireland. Can anything, continued he, be more dreadful than robbing the people of their arms? I told him that the people considered it as the highest act of insult and injustice. Injustice, said he, it is both injustice and ingratitude to the bravest nation on earth. What have the people to expect now? Well, said he, smiling, all ground of jealousy between us and the catholics is now done away with. They have denied us reform and them emancipation; they would not allow them to get arms nor us to keep ours; they have oppressed THEM with penal laws and US with military ones; we are all equally subject to the tender, to dungeons, and to death. Well, said I, it is likely that common sufferings will beget a common interest and a common cause. There is nothing surer, said he, than that IRISHMEN OF EVERY DENOMINATION MUST NOW STAND OR FALL TOGETHER. At saying these words, his companion came up, and said it would be necessary for them now to retire.

EXTRACT OF A LETTER WRITTEN BY ALEXANDER HENRY HALIDAY
TO LORD CHARLEMONT.

"6th October, 1797,
Mount-Stewart.

"It is true three yeomen have been sentenced for two horrid murders, but they have not yet suffered, and are recommended to mercy, while every exertion has been made by most respectable people, and on strong grounds, to save one Orr, or to obtain a mitigation of his punishment, notwithstanding which he will, I believe, be hanged to-morrow at Carrickfergus, leaving behind him a character without reproach (except of this one offence of tendering the united oath, which there is good reason to think he did not do, though he certainly was present, to two fencibles) a heart-broken wife, and six helpless children. Our dear countess [Londonderry, sister of viceroy Camden] has done all it was possible for her to do, but, as it appears at present, with as little success as the rest."

. . . .

"That unfortunate Orr feels aggravated distress from this three days' respite, as it is understood that nothing better is to follow. He had fully prepared himself to die on this day, and had suffered the bitterness of death in taking leave of his wife, children, and friends, so that the persevering efforts of the humane have produced an enhancement, in place of a mitigation, of his punishment. My good old friend, Yelverton, I find this instant has recommended a farther respite of a week. Surely more than protracted torture is intended."

This letter was written under the roof of "our dear countess" Londonderry, and can be taken for what it is worth. Castlereagh could, by the lifting of his finger, have saved the lives of William Orr or his own presbyterian minister, James Porter, of Greyabbey, and others innumerable, had he so willed it, but that was not his policy.

On the evening preceding the day fixed for the execution, a messenger arrived from the castle to the high sheriff. It was considered now as a matter of certainty that he was the messenger of mercy; but when, on the contrary, it was known that he had brought orders for immediate execution, the effect produced upon the anxious public is much more easily imagined than described. On Saturday morning, the 14th October, he was brought out from the gaol, in which he had consumed the last year of his existence, and though his complexion was somewhat altered from the glow of health which it formerly wore, the more than ordinary comeliness of his countenance still remained. His stature was fully six feet, his person graceful, but extremely athletic, and of those proportions which indicate the greatest degree of bodily activity and strength; but, above all, there was in his aspect a mixture of firmness and sensibility which seemed to show him gifted by nature with a generous and elevated spirit. The character he had borne amongst his neighbours confirmed this impression, for he was beloved by all; and in the relations of private life, as a father and a husband, his conduct was amiable and exemplary. When he understood he was to be indulged in a post-chaise to convey him to the place of execution, being apprehensive that he might have soldiers for his companions, he seemed more desirous to walk, in order to enjoy the company of the two clergymen, William Stavely and Adam Hill, whom he had requested to attend him, but these gentlemen being permitted to go with him in the carriage, he arrived at the place of execution about one o'clock, escorted by a very strong military guard, composed of horse, foot, and artillery detached from different regiments in Belfast and Carrickfergus.

43

At the place of execution the infantry were drawn up in a triangular form round the gallows, on the outside of which the cavalry continued to move, whilst at some little distance two field-pieces were planted, ranging with the roads from Carrickfergus and Belfast. But this precaution was unnecessary, as the public seemed rather to shun the spectacle. A few of his particular friends having asked leave to come within the space for the purpose of carrying away his remains were permitted by the sheriff. The prisoner, after employing some time in prayer, sung some few verses of the 23rd Psalm, and seemed to dwell upon the 4th verse:—

> " Yea, tho' I walk in death's dark vale,
> Yet will I fear none ill,"

and he read some verses of the 31st Psalm, repeating emphatically—

> " In thee, O Lord, I put my trust,
> Shamed let me never be."

And also,

> " And sith thou art my strength therefore
> Pull me out of the net,
> Which they in subtility for me
> So privily have set."

> " Unto thy hands I do commit
> My spirit, for thou art he,
> O thou, Jehovah, God of truth,
> That hast redeemed me."

After which he read from the 1st Corinthians, chapter xvi., from the 54th verse to the end, the following passages,

> " So when this corruptible shall have put on incorruption, and this mortal shall have put on
> " immortality, then shall be brought to pass the saying, death is swallowed up in victory."

> " O death, where is thy sting ? O grave, where is thy victory ?
> " The sting of death is sin, and the strength of sin is the law."
> " Therefore my beloved brethren, be ye stedfast, unmoveable   .   .   .   .

He then addressed all who stood near, as well his friends as the military officers and privates, who crowded round him, and loudly and ardently declared his innocence, the falsehood of the prosecutor, and also of a newspaper publication stating that he had acknowledged the justice of his sentence and confessed his guilt. To guard against future calumnies, when he should be no longer in this world to contradict them, he had procured a few printed copies of a just and true declaration, the original of which, in his own writing, he had deposited in the hands of the reverend John Savage, the clergyman who had attended him in gaol, during that period when he found it necessary to prepare himself for eternity. He then distributed a considerable number of printed papers, remonstrating calmly with those who seemed eager to snatch away too many, and observing that by dividing them equally there would be enough to satisfy the curiosity of all. He then shook hands with his friends, took leave of the two clergymen who attended him, and mounted the scaffold with a firm step ; and after the executioner had put the rope about his neck, and when he awaited only the last fatal movement, he gave a preconcerted signal with his handkerchief ; and here, for the first time, discovered some appearance of indignation, exclaiming, "I am no traitor. I die a persecuted man for a persecuted country. Great Jehovah, receive my soul. I die in the true faith of a presbyterian."

In the heathen world less heroic magnanimity would have been Deified ; or, in the early ages of Christianity, less divinity would have been Canonized.

The fine indignation of Orr clearly shows his noble nature when he refused to travel in the coach to his execution with rude soldiers, whose every action must have galled him when he wished to think of other subjects more congenial to his soul. He felt they were but the hackles in a machine set going by those in authority, and their close presence might distract the thoughts of peace in his bosom and the forgiveness of his persecutors as he was led a lamb to the slaughter.

THE EXECUTION OF WILLIAM ORR AT THE GALLOWS GREEN OF CARRICKFERGUS,
14TH OCTOBER, 1797.

The Dying Declaration

OF

WILLIAM ORR,

Of Farranshane, in the County of Antrim, Farmer.

TO THE PUBLIC,—MY FRIENDS AND COUNTRYMEN :—In the Thirty-first year
of my Life, I have been sentenced to die upon the Gallows, and this Sentence
has been in pursuance of a Verdict of Twelve men, who should have been
indifferently and impartially chosen; how far they have been so, I leave to
that Country from which they have been chosen to determine; and how far they
have discharged their Duty, I leave to their God and to themselves.—They
have, in pronouncing their verdict, thought proper to recommend me as an
Object of humane Mercy; in return, I pray to God, if they have erred, to have
Mercy upon them. The Judge, who condemned me, humanely shed tears in
uttering my Sentence; but whether he did wisely, in so highly commending the
wretched Informer, who swore away my Life, I leave to his own cool reflection,
solemnly assuring him and all the World, with my dying Breath, that the
Informer was forsworn. The Law under which I suffer is surely a severe
one; may the Makers and Promoters of it be justified in the Integrity of their
Motives and the Purity of their own Lives—by that Law, I am stamped a
Felon, but my heart disdains the Imputation. My comfortable Lot and
Industrious Course of Life best refute the Charge of being an Adventurer for
Plunder; but if to have loved my Country, to have known its Wrongs, to have
felt the Injuries of the persecuted Catholics, and to have united with them and
all other Religious Persuasions, in the most orderly and least sanguinary Means
of procuring Redress;—If these be Felonies, I am a Felon, but not otherwise.
Had my Counsel (for whose honourable Exertions I am indebted) prevailed in
their Motion to have me tried for High Treason, rather than under the
Insurrection Law, I should have been entitled then to a full Defence and my
Actions and Intentions have been better vindicated; but that was refused, and
I must now submit to what has passed.

To the generous Protection of my Country, I leave a beloved Wife, who has
been constant and true to me, and whose Grief for my fate has already nearly
occasioned her Death. I leave five living Children, who have been my Delight—
may they love their Country as I have done, and die for it, if needful.

Lastly, a false and ungenerous Publication having appeared in a Newspaper, stating certain alleged Confessions of Guilt on my Part, and thus striking
at my Reputation, which is dearer to me than Life, I take this solemn Method
of contradicting that Calumny,—I was applied to by the High Sheriff, and
the Rev. William Bristow, Sovereign of Belfast, to make a confession of guilt,
who used entreaties to that effect; this I peremptorily refused; did I think
myself guilty, I should be free to confess it, but, on the contrary, I glory in my
Innocence.

I trust that all my virtuous countrymen will bear me in their kind remembrance, and continue true and faithful to each other, as I have been to all of them. With this last Wish of my Heart, nothing doubting of the Success of that Cause for which I suffer, and hoping for God's merciful Forgiveness of such Offences as my frail Nature may have at any Time betrayed me into, I die in Peace and Charity with all Mankind.

WILLIAM ORR.

Carrickfergus Gaol, 5 October, 1797.

EXTRACT OF A LETTER FROM CARRICKFERGUS, 14th OCTOBER, 1797.

"The inhabitants of this town, man, woman, and child, quit the place this day, rather than be present at the execution of their hapless countryman, William Orr. Some removed to a distance of many miles—scarce a sentence was interchanged during the day, and every face presented a picture of the deepest melancholy, horror and indignation. The military who attended the execution consisted of several thousand men, horse and foot, with cannon, and a company of artillery —the whole forming a hollow square. To these William Orr read his dying declaration, with a clear, strong, manly tone of voice—and his deportment was firm, unshaken and impressive, to the last instant of his existence. He was a dissenter, of exemplary morals, and of most industrious habits ; and in the characters of husband, father and neighbour, eminently amiable and respected· The love he bore his country was pure, ardent, and disinterested—spurning all religious distinctions ; and his last accents articulated the prophetic hope that Ireland would soon be emancipated."

A small circumstance worthy of note occurred shortly before his alighting from the carriage. A poor man who was his tenant, stood weeping by his side, to whom he stretched out his hat, which he presented to him as a token of friendship and remembrance, and requested his friends to shew kindness to him, for though he was poor he was honest, which was more to be respected than wealth.

This man was Davey MacQuillin, who farmed a small portion, about 13 acres, of the lands of Farranshane, and was a personal friend of William Orr. He is buried in Dunagore churchyard. The MacQuillin's treasured greatly a silver badge of the ANTRIM VOLUNTEERS, the epauletts and scarf made of silver wire, also three silver buckles. These articles are Irish hall-marked, and, I believe, were Orr's. After the death of the last MacQuillin they came into my possession. These volunteer relics belonged to an officer and would not probably belong to the MacQuillin's. Personally, this belief and the way they were prized, and so long retained, confirm me in my opinion that they were William Orr's, especially as we know the friendship and esteem he had for Davey MacQuillin, and his desire to confer a favour upon him.

The gallows green at Carrickfergus had witnessed many a sight, but never such as this. Thousands of troops crowded the shore, flanked with artillery, to overawe and break the spirit of the people, and show what power could do. Had not the viceroy decreed it with all the facts before him, knowing it was a gross miscarriage of justice ? Had not his wife been implored with words that would have melted the heart of any woman that ever bore a child ? Silent and sullen the people had left the place—had withdrawn themselves like the sun behind the dark cloud that overshadowed the land.

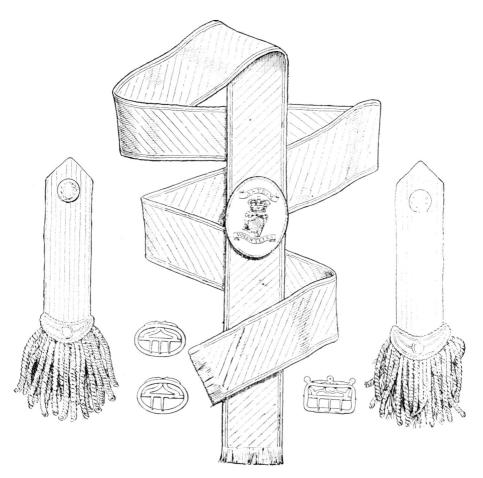

RELICS OF THE ANTRIM VOLUNTEERS BELONGING TO WILLIAM ORR.

48

"Therefore, my brethren, be ye stedfast, unmoveable;" and the firm step and proud mien of an innocent man bore him to the scaffold, and then he hurled his last defiant words at his executioners.

" I am no traitor, I die a persecuted man, for a persecuted country."

No one envies the thoughts of the Macartneys, or of Skeffington, or Bristow, or Wolfe, or Yelverton, or Castlereagh, or Camden, as the horror of this tragedy was borne in upon them, and the ever haunting thought of the parts they had played in bringing to pass such a scene outside the walls of Carrickfergus.

It has been stated that William Orr at the time of his execution gave his hat and his watch as mementoes to this "poor tenant who was a catholic." I cannot get this latter statement corroborated, as Davey MacQuillin was a presbyterian, and was so buried. He doubtless came of a catholic stock judging by his name, and this may have given rise to the statement. I also believe the MacQuillins to have been a remnant of the "mere Irish" left after the plantation had swept over the country, and that they clung to their old patrimony, even as under-tenants. The MacQuillins had been lords of Rathmor of Magh-linne, and their great rath is still preserved close beside Farranshane. William Orr, knowing this, may have had a special affection for one of the old stock.

As was usual after an execution, the body was taken from the gallows to a neighbouring house, and every means adopted for the restoration of life, including bleeding, but without avail, as the neck was broken. The hangman had done his work completely, as well as his masters desired. The house still stands: it was called " Wilson's slate house," after a man of that name who was its occupier. It is on the land side of the road opposite the gallows green. The body was then placed on a cart, bedded with straw, and a start made for its long home. Then it was that the friends began to gather, so that long before Ballynure was reached the country side was black with the vast concourse of people, in every heart a throb and in every eye a tear—mourners every one of them in the fullest sense of the term; mourners for their mangled brother, mourners for their bleeding country. People rushed from their houses to wait on the roadside in tears and anguish while the corpse was carried past. One man named Kennedy stepped forward and kissed the bier. Many others did likewise.

The corpse was borne by the road up the mountain side, past Duncrue, over Briantang brae, and across the commons of Carrickfergus, through Straid to Ballynure, which was reached as dusk had fallen on that gloomy October day. Here a halt was made at the meeting-house, where the body was dressed and coffined, and the wake held. The meeting-house was in the centre of the village of Ballynure, and adjoined the residence of Hughey Fullarton. He was a strong united man, a reed maker to trade, and a teacher

49

of the children of the surrounding farmers, who assembled in the little room at the rere of the meeting-house. Orr's friend and spiritual consoler, Adam Hill, was preacher in Ballynure. To the west of the meeting-house was the old parish school, then came the pound with a stream of water running through it. For allowing the wake to take place in his meeting-house, it is said Adam Hill was arrested and lodged in Carrick jail. The Ballynure poet, William Campbell, was similarly treated for the sympathy he showed. Hill was released because no one was forthcoming to identify him. One witness, a presbyterian soldier, to save his

THE WAKE OF WILLIAM ORR IN THE OLD MEETING-HOUSE IN BALLYNURE,
14 AND 15 OCTOBER, 1797.

(from a drawing by J.W.C.)

clergy, stated the prisoner was not the minister, as he had different coloured hair, and was fair-featured.

The people for miles around, many having come very long distances, remained in Ballynure all night, watching and guarding the dead body with an almost idolatrous care. On the Sunday, the remainder of the journey was taken from Ballynure to Ballyclare, thence along the banks of the Six-mile-water through Ballylinney and the grange of Ballywalter, through Ballyhartfield and Ballycushan, crossing the Ballymartin burn, and so into Templepatrick. The attendance was so vast, and their spirits such as could not have been hastily tampered with, and the military force not of such strength, otherwise the viceroy's proclamation would have been enforced in regard to the funeral, as such gatherings were quite illegal, and positive orders had been issued to the military to suppress them "with their full power." Discretion was doubtless the better part of valour, and so persuasive means were employed to disperse the mourning thousands. The populace was restrained by every means in the power of their leaders from all acts of reprisal, though many such were contemplated. The crowd quietly went to their homes, each one with the thought burnt into his heart, "Remember Orr." The military dissuaded many from going to Templepatrick, getting them to leave at the cross-roads.

As the funeral of William Orr passed from Ballynure to Templepatrick, an amazing concourse of people crowded the road and the adjacent hills. A party of dragoons came out under the command of an officer, who said he had orders to disperse them. To this no opposition was made, but it was found impossible to turn back so great and so compacted a crowd until the procession advanced to a cross-road, where a great number did return; a greater number, however, still continued to flock in till they arrived, but without the least tendency to disorder, at the place of interment. Here, by desire of the officer, who, although strict in the execution of his orders, offered no disrespect to the people, nor received any provocation from them, the select friends alone of William Orr proceeded to the burying-ground, where he was interred, three dragoons on horseback being stationed by his grave.

The strangled corpse of William Orr was laid to rest in the family graveyard at Templepatrick, where a simple stone had been erected to the memory of his favourite sister, Ally (Alicia) Orr, after whom he had called his infant daughter. And so the old churchyard was consecrated afresh, and made a doubly sacred spot for all time when it received the body of William Orr within its fold.

With the prophetic eye we see a few short years later the self-mangled corpse of him who had helped to bring this all to pass hooted, jostled, and jeered as the purple pall that enshrouded the livid throat of Castlereagh was hurried through the portals of Westminster abbey out of the gaze of an angry populace. We must needs moralise—better, far better, the grassy grave beneath the dripping trees of Templepatrick, with a memory enshrined in a people's heart, than a marble grave dug in dishonour and a memory redolent of blood and infamy.

Poor innocent Orr, it would almost appear, thought he had been " tried and convicted." Orr was never tried, the whole thing was a trumped-up political tragedy. The most that can be admitted is that some of those who took part in hounding him to death were perhaps acting unwittingly, just as the Roman soldiers acted. How could it be deemed a " trial " with such prosecutors, such witnesses, such judges, and such a jury ? To give a fair trial the judges must be free men, above suspicion ; the jury should be the tried one's peers, unpacked and unbiassed ; and the evidence not suborned. Orr had no trial—he was judicially murdered to serve a political end with the full connivance of lord Castlereagh and the personal approbation of viceroy Camden, each of them knowing the full purport of his action. He was dubbed a "traitor" for the same purpose. It was not enough to rob him of his life, his very character must be blackened, and at the very moment of his death, facing eternity, he rises to the full dignity of his manhood and defiantly hurls back in the teeth of his murderers, "I am no traitor, I die a persecuted man, for a persecuted country." Never were braver words spoken, nor with more honest vehemence, and truer conviction. There was no cringing to the approaching juggernaut that was to crush out life and everything dear to him, everything but his own proud honour, and that it could not even stain. Every device was used to tarnish it, but the foulness only clings to the memories of those who made the futile effort. The honour of William Orr was dearer to him than life itself—it came to him with no royal prerogative—man did not give it, and man could not

THE BURIAL OF WILLIAM ORR IN TEMPLEPATRICK,
15TH OCTOBER, 1797.

take it from him. It still clings to his memory, and will ever do so whenever his name is mentioned while the world lasts.

Orr's whole life is clearly indicated by his own words, as given by *Humanitas*, and in his letters and dying declaration. These views were carefully written and conned over at the time, and stand out as the indelible truth. Clergymen and officials may say what they like, or try to wriggle out of awkward situations as they choose, but everything they did and said was tainted with ulterior motives. I would place the dying words of William Orr—poured forth in their very face, in view of high heaven itself, when his honour alone remained to him in all the world—I would place the martyr's words before a thousand of their oaths : " If to have loved my country, to have known its wrongs, to have felt the injuries of the persecuted catholics, and to have united with them and all other religious persuasions . . . if these be felonies, then I am a felon, but not otherwise." And this was the " felony" that Orr suffered for. There was no other real charge against him ; to have united all creeds and classes in Ireland was a crime in the eyes of government, its aiders and abettors. Orr saw this when he said, " You may depend upon it that there is some system laid down which has for its object murder and devastation." He saw clearly their system : " Ireland must suffer." Then we have that sterling unanswered prayer of his : " O, if God would give the king wisdom to change the ministry in due time, what a happy thing it would be for the country, what calamity and woe it would prevent." " I wish to God," said he, " that the people of Ireland could obtain their wishes without any assistance from France. . . . I would have connection with none of them, except a connection that would secure to us independence, liberty, and commerce. O, if Ireland was wise and united, she would soon be free and happy." Were ever nobler wishes expressed in nobler language ; how they shine out like stars in the black firmament of statescraft, villainy, and baseness that covered the whole land. The real felons now stand revealed. Whose the treason we all know. Felons to their fellow man and human liberty, reeking with treason to their common country, men who " measured their own consequence by the coffins of their victims." They were the statesmen and crown officials, the clergy, yeomen, and lawyers who tracked to his doom an innocent man like William Orr, falsely using to him and his like such epithets with an intolerant and brazen effrontery.

Orr was appealed to by the high sheriff and William Bristow " to make a confession of guilt, and used entreaties to that effect," but he " peremptorily refused." " I glory in my innocence . . . I die in peace and charity with all mankind." What a triumphant spirit was his, as in a clear, firm voice he read aloud these words beside the scaffold, and beneath the hangman's rope, with its circle of crimson soldiers and glittering steel, flanked with heavy guns—one speck of innocence in a vortex of power, bloody and relentless, with its object " murder and devastation." Truly, the proudest charge on the shield of the Orrs is the hangman's rope, and more to be prized than the coronet of a marquis steeped in blood. Well, indeed, might the whole country " Remember Orr," and in patriotic fervour look upon the gallows green as the national Golgotha outside the walls of Carrickfergus. Many a curse has been muttered, many a hat raised in reverence as the spot has been passed by countless thousands.

Sir Richard Musgrave, baronet, in 1801, in his account of the insurrection, stated that William Orr was attended constantly in jail by father O'Coigly and two presbyterian ministers, " dreading that he would make discoveries, as he had intimated an intention of doing so." This is on a par with all similar statements of Musgrave, absolutely untrue, and known so to be. The priest had, doubtless, never visited Orr, certainly not constantly, and the two ministers were only allowed to see him at intervals, whilst his jailers were in full control of his movements. Every opportunity was afforded Orr to "make discoveries," even to the final persuasions of sheriff Skeffington and vicar Bristow, without any result whatsoever. Orr never dreamed of treachery ; not even to save his own life would he admit any guilt ; and, I believe, not to save his soul would he have turned traitor. On every occasion when Musgrave could traduce the united men he did so ; for truth he had no regard. He was a subsidised government hack, of the most insane rabid order, bitterly violent in the extreme. His own wife, whom he treated barbarously, stated, according to Barrington, that he was " half mad by nature," and one "of the most unfeeling and abominable of fanatics." He states incidentally, however, that "they carried Orr's body to a presbyterian meeting-house, where two medical men endeavoured to restore him to life by transposing the blood of a calf into his veins. Not succeeding, his body was laid out in great state, and he was honoured with a most splendid funeral, which was attended by a numerous body of united Irishmen, who lamented in doleful accents the fate of this martyr to republican liberty, and bedewed his hearse with sympathetic tears."

EXTRACT OF A LETTER FROM CARRICKFERGUS, OCTOBER, 1797.

" While the fate of the unfortunate William Orr was undecided, the public seemed sunk in silent and torpid suspense, but the moment he was no more, a universal sentiment of grief, and horror, and execration resounded from every tongue. One would suppose this wretched people had not been sufficiently familiarized to murder, to burning, to rape, to military massacre, to arbitrary captivity, and to arbitrary banishment; one would think they had ceased to feel for their wretched kindred, their fathers, their brothers, husbands, sons, who are now rotting in jails, or packed up like cargoes of negroes—God knows for what market, or how they may be summarily disposed of on the way. Strange as it may appear, the very soldiery from whom they shrunk as a set of crusaders, sent for the purpose of butchery and rapine, or, as it was well expressed by lord Ancrum's fencibles, who said they would show 'that they were not come here to be trifled with' has acquired a sort of comparative popularity."

General Lake was in the north at this time acting on the written orders of secretary Pelham to "take the most immediate and decisive measures for disposing "of the military force under your command, aided by the yeomanry corps, for "immediately disarming all persons who shall not bear his majesty's commission . . " . . his excellency gives you this full authority in order to give your discretion the "greatest latitude." We know what such orders meant, and how they were enforced by a man like Lake. He it was who won the " races of Castlebar," heading his men in their forty-mile stampede, though they vastly outnumbered the French under Humbert. The French were trained soldiers, however, and not Antrim peasants, so the general certainly gave " his discretion the greatest latitude." We find him reporting to Pelham that Orr's friends had offered a bribe of £900 to the jailer to allow his escape. There was doubtless no truth in this, for to the last the friends of the doomed man never believed he was to be sacrificed, so the general was only repeating or making gossip to show the importance of the prisoner, and to prove how safely he was guarded. Orr would likely have been free if that amount of hard cash had been forthcoming. Lecky describes Lake acting " now, as ever, with a brutal, stupid, and indiscriminating severity."

The nation was thunderstruck at the decision of lord Camden that Orr must hang. The *London Courier* commenced an article regarding the execution, " Murder most foul." Drennan's ode fired the feelings of the people with a righteous rage. His memory was toasted by thousands. " The memory of Orr, basely murdered," " May the execution of Orr provide places for the cabinet of saint James at the castle," " That the Irish cabinet soon take the place of William Orr," were the toasts given at a public banquet given to C. J. Fox, on his birthday, when lord Norfolk, lord Oxford, Erskine, sir Francis Burdett, and Horne Tooke were present, " Remember Orr " were the last words on the manifesto which doomed the faithful brothers Sheares. They ended the memorial card of the " Soldiers four," or " Death before dishonour." A man at Hillsborough was hanged for having the same words on a token hidden in his shoe. It was the rallying cry at every gathering, stimulating thousands by the thoughts it conjured up. It echoed and re-echoed from the insurgent ranks at the battle of Antrim. It was heard at Saintfield and Ballynahinch, and at every other spot where there was any number of united men.

Small portions of the crape with which Orr's eyes were covered at his execution were treasured by his countrymen, memorial cards were printed and circulated everywhere. Little pink rosettes of silk, with an inscription printed around a harp,

SILK ROSETTE IN MEMORY OF WILLIAM ORR.

were distributed. This inscription might well be called the song of the Niobe of the nations. It was penned by a masterhand, by· one who felt keenly what he wrote. It is worthy of a place side by side with the finest lamentations in scripture. Whose was the heart that thought it—whose was the pen that wrote it? I have one of these little mementos, which I dearly prize. The following is the wording :—

"Sad is the sleep of Erin, and her dreams are troubled and gloomy. Her enemy has come—he has come in the hour of her slumber, and his hand has stolen the EMERALD from her brow; but Erin has not awakened—no, she still sleeps.

Bloody is the field where she lies, and her garments are weeping with blood— for the wounds of her sons are streaming around her, and the ghosts of her heroes are moaning for vengeance; but Erin has not awakened—no, she still sleeps.

A sigh comes on the night breeze—'tis the spirit of Orr that complains; pensive he leans from his cloud, and weeps over the slumber of Erin. He touches the lyre of song; the heavenly harp of union—and the orisons of freedom tremble over the chords—'twas a strain he loved, for he "DIED SINGING IT." Has Erin heard the voice of her hero? Has Erin awakened? No, she still sleeps."

I have also another little white silk rosette, in the centre of which is

Orr

and the

14th October,

1797.

SILK ROSETTE
IN MEMORY OF WILLIAM ORR.

And around this—

"Irishmen, let us bear him in steadfast Memory—Let HIS fate nerve the martial arm to wreck the wrongs of ERIN—and assert her undoubted claims:—Let ORR be the watch-word to LIBERTY!"

Tokens bore the words, Remember Orr—it was found written on the walls, and on the pavements. It was cut on pike handles, it was in the mouth of everyone.

The most valued of all these relics in my possession, is a little thin finger or scarf ring, hand-made, of gold. On one side is a round plate enclosing a green enamelled shamrock, with white enamel surrounding it. On the opposite side in an oval are the words, "Remember Orr," and on each side of the plate in gaelic letters eɲɲ ʒo bɲᴀʒh. Engraved inside are the letters "presented by Robert Orr." This is one of the rings so frequently referred as having been made at the time, but I know of no other example now to the fore. It was given by William Orr's widow and daughter to William Stevenson, of Spring-field, Belfast, who had befriended the family at Farranshane in many ways, and was a regular visitor there, and from his descendant it came to me. It has been repaired in several places, the explanation being that it was smashed in pieces by Orr's daughter, and then thrown away to hide it from the eyes of the soldiers, who were on the look out for such "treasonable" articles, as its possession was made an offence punishable by death.

MEMORIAL RING FOR WILLIAM ORR.

One of these rings was given by Henry Joy MacCracken to his sister Mary, as a token for his mother, immediately after his arrest, when he was in Carrick jail, where William Orr had been imprisoned. MacCracken had worn it at Antrim, and valued it highly. After his death, it was treasured by his mother during life, and afterwards by his faithful sister.

The sword of William Orr is at Farranshane, in the possession of a relation— the bayonet of his gun is in the possession of the writer.

THE SWORD, SHEATH, AND BAYONET OF WILLIAM ORR.

Memorial cards were also printed in considerable quantities, and highly prized.

The printers of these cards, and also of the dying declaration, ran great risks from military raids as recorded further on, but the risk was freely run all the same. The following is a fac-simile of one of these cards.

To the Memory of

WILLIAM ORR,

Who was offer'd up at Carrickfergus, on Saturday,
the 14th of October, 1797 :
an awful sacrifice to

IRISH FREEDOM,

on the *Altar* of *British Tyranny*,
by the hands of *Perjury*,
thro' the influence of *Corruption*
and the Connivance of

PARTIAL JUSTICE !!

O ! Children of ERIN ! when ye *forget* HIM,
his Wrongs, his death, his Cause,
the injur'd RIGHTS of MAN ;
nor these revenge :—

May you be debar'd THAT LIBERTY he sought,
and *forgotten* in the Hist'ry of Nations ;
or, if remember'd,
remember'd with disgust and execration,
or nam'd with scorn and horror !

No, Irishmen ! let us bear him in steadfast Memory ;
Let HIS fate nerve the martial arm
to wreak the Wrongs of

ERIN,

and assert her undoubted Claims :—
Let ORR be the watch-word to LIBERTY !

FACSIMILE OF THE WILLIAM ORR MEMORIAL CARD.

A gloom settled down on William Orr's desolated home at Farranshane, only disturbed by the cries of the orphan children for the kind parent who never returned to dandle them on his knees, or assist in their little sports and pastimes. They saddened for life the heart of their mother with their eager questions, "Will father never come home?" "Why does he stay away so long?" and "Why are you always sad, mother?"

> They wonder "Why he keeps away?"
> But by and bye "he will come home."
> They talk of him the livelong day,
> And ask her, "Will he never come?"—R. R. M.

In the spring-time her baby came with the cherry blossoms, a fatherless bairn ushered into the world, into a house of gloom and sadness, when all should have been joy and light-heartedness. Viceroy Camden "feasting in his castle in the midst of his myrmidons and bishops" must surely have seen, as there is a God above, the handwriting on the wall.

Through the dreary winter months after the execution Isabella Orr had often passed along the sodden roads and under the dripping trees to castle Upton to her husband's new made grave, to bedew the sod with her tears, and place some simple token of her love upon the mound that covered him who was so dear to her.

Little Wilhemina was but seven weeks old when the fight at Antrim took place. From Farranshane the din of battle could be easily heard, and the smoke of the artillery seen above the town. How the widowed mother must have held her breath that day, gathering her little flock close around her, scarce tasting food, such was her anxiety and dread. Many friends and neighbours called with her that sunny June morning as they hurried to the place of meeting, with their bright keen pikes glistening on their shoulders, telling her that all would be well, that such a blow would be struck that day as would for ever vindicate the fair fame of her dead husband, and cast into utter confusion those who had conspired to take his life. One waited for another at the corner of the boreen until a little clump had gathered, and then with a shout, "Come on boys, and remember Orr," they hurriedly passed on to join their comrades. In the evening terror seized her as first one, then another, then a group, and finally a great mass of insurgents retreated from Antrim town broken, but not disordered, when she well knew the day had been lost. Eagerly she watched as the remnant of them clustered on the heights of Dunagore, and hastily threw up their entrenchments for a last stand, and then she prepared for the worst. The flashing of helmets and glinting of red coats was seen through the trees as she hurriedly made for the burn braes, dragging her little ones with her, to hide amongst the whins and briers. The yeomen plundered and sacked the house of all its belongings, one wrangled with another for what he most fancied, what they could not carry away they smashed in their wicked fury. Amongst the many plunderers was one who stole the eight-day clock that had long struck the hours for the Orrs. Some years afterwards he like many of his comrades came to beggary, and his goods were sold, when the old clock was returned to Farranshane, where it is at this day. Not satisfied with plunder they, must needs fire the homestead and poor widow Orr from her hiding-place, with only God's earth beneath her feet and His sky overhead, saw the flames of her roof tree redden the summer sky, and then she knew that the very worst that man could do had been done, and she would fain have lain down and died. A mother's love for her children alone sustained her, and so she braced

THE HIDING-PLACE OF WIDOW ORR AND HER CHILDREN
AT THE BURN BRAES, FARRANSHANE.

herself to the struggle for their sake. For many days she lived at the braes in terror, crouching with her little ones in a rude sheiling under the overhanging thorns. She also sought shelter under the banks of the burn in Ballyno, an adjoining townland. Here a kind neighbour sought her out, and went with her to Henry Adair, a local magistrate, who, it is said, obtained permission for her to return to her charred and desolate home.

She weeps not, though the scene is sad,
The cheerful circle wrapped in gloom,
The house where all of late looked glad,
A dismal home—a living tomb.—R.R.M.

For weeks afterwards the smell of burnt meal was felt at Farranshane, as the house was a full one and well stored. In time an older house adjoining was fitted up for her, and here she lived for many years, chastened and saddened by so many trials. Truly her path was a *via dolorosa*. She was described to me as "a small, quiet, beautiful woman, who never took heart after the troubles." She visited friends very seldom, her husband's grave she went to see at times, and on Sundays she walked to meeting in Antrim.

Neighbours and friends were very good to her, lowering their voices when her name was mentioned, and ever the eye moistened at the thought of "William Orr's

THE OLD MEETING-HOUSE IN ANTRIM WHERE THE ORRS WORSHIPPED.
(Previous to restoration, from a sketch by F. W. Lockwood.)

widow and weans." Ploughing was done, and the harvest was gleaned for her; six hundred neighbours assembled on one occasion when Orr was still alive, and cut down all the corn, and gathered in the crops in a few hours. At the first of these gatherings all sorts of people were present, many of the wealthy driving there in their chaises — the machines lined the road for half a mile — well dressed women vieing with each other who could gather the most in their silk aprons. Andy Parker, of Rathbeg, organised such parties, so that neither potatoes or corn suffered while Orr was in jail, nor after his execution.

Actions like these served to cheer and brighten the sad, sad days through which widow Orr had to pass. These kindly actions of her neighbours were done in open defiance of the law, for Camden's vice-regal proclamation warned all persons not to take part in such actions, giving power to his majesty's troops " by the exertions of their utmost force to suppress the same." The charitable act was thus armed with daring and bravery.

Isabella Orr died in the long, low thatched house that had been fitted up for her after the burning of her husband's home. She died and was waked in the bedroom off the room to the right of the door.

THE HOUSE AT FARRANSHANE WHERE WILLIAM ORR'S WIDOW LIVED AND DIED.

Her sorrows are numbered—no longer she weeps—
Every pang she endured is requited ;
With endless delight, and in silence she sleeps,
For in death with her love she's united.—(ANON.)

Her son, major John Orr, was very attentive to her in her last illness, staying in MacAnally's hotel in Antrim, not to give any trouble in the house, and walking over by the lane every day, to be with her and comfort her. When she died, he performed the death duties with his own hands.

She died in the forties and was buried beside her husband in Templepatrick. Many old friends and some new ones gathered to her funeral as it crept along the old road under Dunagore past the scenes of her life's tragedy. An eye-witness told me that there was a goodly gathering, all, save one, in coaches or on horseback. Her life and her fate had brought around her many true friends—honest and true—not timeservers or placehunters.

Major Orr had served with distinction in the Peninsula war, having obtained a commission when he was twenty-three. Some one in authority had taken this dubious way of trying to make some reparation. When he returned to England in 1817, the duke of York complimented him upon his services, and then asked him if there was any promotion he desired. "I hate the sword I wear;" was Orr's reply, "perhaps your royal highness will allow me to retire from the service?" "Pray, are you related to Orr who suffered in '98 ? " said the duke. "I have the honour to be his son," Orr replied. His resignation was accepted, and £1000 was sent to his widowed mother as some slight compensation for the loss she had sustained twenty years before.

Of William Orr's two brothers, James and Samuel, the former lived at Ballymena, leaving, amongst other descendants, the present county court judge, James Orr. Samuel lived at Harp hall, and led a contingent at the battle of Antrim. His descendants are at present in occupation of Farranshane. William Orr has left no male descendants, but a daughter of his son John still survives in London, and she has two sons. It is said that James Orr, the poet of Ballycarry, the writer of the well-known ballad, "The Irishman," was a cousin of William Orr.

During the time between the sentence and the execution of William Orr, when every effort was made to gain a respite of the sentence, a remarkable position was created by the actions of the high sheriff, Chichester Skeffington, the vicar and sovereign of Belfast, William Bristow, who was also a very active magistrate, and others. The whole position can be best understood from the newspaper correspondence which appeared at the time.

The following appeared in the *Belfast News-Letter* :—

TO THE PUBLIC.

It is with extreme reluctance that we address the public on so distressing a subject, but having seen a printed paper, signed William Orr, which was delivered by him yesterday, as his dying declaration at the place of his execution, in which was this assertion, viz., " I was applied to by the high sheriff and the reverend William Bristow, sovereign of Belfast, to make a confession of guilt, who used entreaties to that effect, this I peremptorily refused."

We think it a duty we owe to ourselves and the public, to state precisely the purport of our conversation with the unfortunate man on the subject alluded to in his declaration, and the circumstances that led to it.

Being at Carrickfergus on Wednesday, the 27th September, to attend an election of an alderman and burgess for that corporation, the sheriff expressed an intention of going into the gaol for the purpose of seeing if the prisoner (William Orr) had every reasonable accommodation that his unfortunate position would admit of, and requested the reverend William Bristow to accompany him. After some enquiries from the prisoner to that effect, and some observations on a religious book, which William Orr had been reading, the reverend Bristow said to him, "Sir, I have seen a paper which your brother and another gentleman brought to the sheriff on Monday last, with your name annexed to it, in which you acknowledge the justness of your sentence, and cautioned others against being led into bad practices by wicked and designing men." The reverend Bristow added, "that it was expected, from what your brother and that gentleman told the sheriff, that it would have been published in last Monday's Belfast paper. I am confident, said the reverend Bristow to William Orr, that this acknowledgement, which you had for some time withheld, must now afford you great comfort." William Orr replied, "Yes, sir, it has relieved my mind very much." The reverend Bristow then said to William Orr, "As you are conscious of your guilt, it is your bounden duty if you know of any conspiracy against the state, to make a discovery of any circumstances you may know which can throw any light upon it, as the only reparation you can make to your injured country." William Orr replied, "I can recollect none at present." The sheriff then said, "William Orr, if upon reflection you should hereafter recollect any circumstances of that nature which you would wish to communicate, I will, upon your application, immediately attend you, or the reverend Bristow, I am certain, will do so, or any other magistrate of the county." William Orr replied, "I thank you, sir."

This we affirm was the whole substance of what then passed between us and the unfortunate William Orr, and as nearly as we can recollect, the exact words, and that we never had a conversation with him on that subject at any other time.

The truth of this whole statement we are ready (if necessary) to attest in the most solemn manner.

C. SKEFFINGTON,
high sheriff of the county of Antrim.
WILLIAM BRISTOW,
sovereign of Belfast.

BELFAST,
   15th October, 1797.

TO THE PUBLIC.

In consequence of seeing a paragraph in the Belfast news-paper signed by Chichester Skeffington, high sheriff of the co. of Antrim, and the rev. William Bristow, sovereign of Belfast, relative to the declaration of my late brother, I am therefore induced, in justice to the character of my brother and myself, to lay the whole of that transaction before the public. A few days after my brother was found guilty and sentenced to die, I went to Belfast and applied to many gentlemen for the purpose of using their interest to have the punishment of my brother mitigated, and in the presence of James Dickey, of Randalstown, and Thomas L. Stewart, of Belfast, I applied to John Staples, a member of parliament for this county, and the hon. Wm. John Skeffington, for the above purpose, who proposed, if I would get a written confession of guilt from my brother, that they would sign a memorial for the purpose of obtaining his pardon, and the hon. Wm. John Skeffington said "he would go round the gentlemen of the grand jury, who were then mostly in Belfast, and get the memorial signed by them." In consequence of which I got a written confession prepared before I left Belfast, and produced it to the hon. Wm. John Skeffington, and asked him if it was full enough, to which he agreed. I accordingly went to Carrickfergus and applied to my brother to sign the confession which I produced to him, telling him "if he would sign it the above gentlemen would sign a memorial to obtain his pardon, and get the rest of the grand jury to do so." On his reading the written confession, he declared "he never would consent to sign a paper

64

acknowledging his guilt and the justice of his sentence, as he was not guilty of the crime he was charged with." Not being able to induce him to consent to the above, I left him ; and conceiving it would be of very material use, and be the means of saving his life—for this purpose, and through that view I signed in his name the confession of guilt, entirely without the privity or consent of my brother, and immediately returned to Belfast, and delivered it to the hon. Wm. John Skeffington as the act of my brother, with which I believe he went round to the above gentlemen, in order to obtain their signatures to the memorial, which they refused. This was the only transaction, being entirely my act, and not that of my brother, as he utterly refused. This I am ready to verify upon oath.

Cranfield, October 17, 1797.   JAMES ORR.

FROM THE *BELFAST NEWS-LETTER* OF 27 OCT., 1797.

Having seen a paragraph in the *Belfast News-Letter*, signed JAMES ORR, stating that I had promised to sign a memorial to the Lord Lieutenant in order to obtain a pardon for his brother, then under sentence of death, on condition that he made a written confession of his guilt, I think it necessary thus publicly to declare that I never made any such promise. I did recommend it to him to prevail on his brother to make and publish a full confession of his guilt, and with it an exhortation to the deluded people with whom he had been connected to desist from their wicked and treasonable pursuits, as the only possible chance he had for mercy. Since the morning on which that conversation passed I have never seen or heard from any of the parties present relative to the subject above mentioned.

23 October, 1797.   JOHN STAPLES.

THE FOLLOWING EXTRACTS ARE FROM THE *PRESS*.

Here then the black conspiracy comes out. To execute a sentence of death, founded on a verdict impeached on the oaths of two of the jury who found it, as obtained under the influence of drunkenness and terror, and upon the evidence of a witness who, in the bitterness of his remorse, declares his perjury, would have been too unseemly a procedure even in the pursuit of a favourite victim, and therefore an offer of mercy is held out, but the price of that mercy is to be the confession of guilt—and a brother, armed with all the force of fraternal affection, and the cries and prayers of a beloved wife and children, is sent as the advocate to exact that confession to save a brother's life. But now we see, by the testimony of that brother, that the manly and virtuous victim scorned to purchase the boon of mercy at such a price. His brother, distracted between grief and affection, supplies the defect, and subscribes to the confession of guilt, little aware that instead of thereby saving his brother's life he was sealing his doom.

And this surreptitious declaration, thus swindled from the fears of an afflicted family, is made an instrument to intercept the stream of mercy and counteract even the report of the judge who tried him, and the disposition of that executive power who is bound to execute justice with mercy.

The actors in the foul conspiracy against the life and character of this devoted victim are not content to let the FOETID fame of their black actions ROT into oblivion, but by attempting to justify themselves under specious appearances, and surreptitious testimonies, they tempt us to such investigation as shall make

"THIS FOUL DEED TO SMELL ABOVE THE EARTH,

"LIKE CARRION MEN GROANING FOR BURIAL."

To villify the veracity of a man, honourable and upright through life, in his last and solemn declaration, and implicate him in the guilt of murdering his own character—to weave for his persecutors a mantle of innocence, and cover the stains of his blood indelible from their hands, a bold and flagitious assertion is made in *Faulkner's Journal* and the *Belfast News-Letter*, " that the devoted William Orr confessed his guilt, and acknowledged the justice of his sentence," and to bolster this impudent lie, the letter of the hon. Chichester Skeffington and the reverend William Bristow is brought forward, and afterwards backed with their affidavit by way of CODICIL.

But what do these gentlemen assert? that they came abruptly, through curiosity, into the cell where William Orr awaited the execution of an ignominious sentence that was to stamp his memory with disgrace, and tear him for ever from an amiable and affectionate wife and five darling children, and from family, friends, and connections, with whom he lived in long and mutual intercourse of esteem and respect.

They found him, they say, reading a religious book, most probably absorbed in deep and melancholy reflection, struggling to reconcile the feelings of nature to the dictates of religion, and to resign himself with manly calmness to his hard, hard fate.

They protrude upon him abrupt and insulting questions—they talk to him of a paper SIGNED WITH HIS NAME, which they saw in the hands of the sheriff, acknowledging his guilt—they congratulate him on the consoling peace of conscience such a confession must have yielded, and they state a dialogue between William Orr and them, couching, however, their statement under this cautious salvo, "OR WORDS TO THAT EFFECT." Now let any man candidly read the answers of William Orr, as stated by them, and ask his judgment whether they do not appear to be rather the discreet and passive responses of a man in his awful situation displeased with the cruelty and impertinence of such an obtrusion, but wishing to get rid of his visitants as civilly and speedily as possible, rather than as anything that could be fairly construed into a confession of guilt.

But Chichester Skeffington, William Bristow, or anybody may state what conversation they please with the unfortunate William Orr. They have not him to confront them: for, alas, he is gone "to the bourne, from whence no traveller returns." But to his last solemn declaration we now add the declaration of his brother as an indelible record against them. The candid public may then be fairly asked,

" UTRUM HORUM MAVIS ACCIPUS,"

for our parts we will, as Hamlet says, " take the ghost's word for a thousand."

We have authority to say that the statement, which appeared in the Dublin papers, of William Orr having made a confession of guilt, is from beginning to end false. That account originated in the *Belfast News-Letter*, a paper generally known to be under court influence.

There is something unutterably heinous in the meditation to ratify the doom of an unfortunate man, when under sentence of death. A forgery to this purpose, is the blackest and foulest of all forgeries. Imagination cannot conceive a more hellish malignity, than that of thus bearing false witness after trial, in order to close the grasp of the executioner upon his victim.

Several prints of Dublin have copied from the *Belfast News-Letter*, which stated that William Orr had made a confession of guilt—only one of them (the *Hibernian*) has had the honour to retract from the error. They have lent their arm to the stroke of the assassin publicly, and they now go moping about in the dark, and whispering every one that they meet, such was the fact. Nothing can be more false. William Orr made no such confession. An innocent or an honest man could have no such confession to make. The confessions are all on the other side. The prosecutor has confessed that he had sworn falsely—the jury have confessed that they acted inconsiderately—and for our part, we confess, that as circumstances appear, should William Orr suffer, going out of the world he might say, in the language of the Messiah—"Forgive them, Father, for they know not what they do."

It may be mentioned here that the Dublin papers, *Faulkner's Journal* and the *Freeman*, were both heavily subsidised by government. The latter was owned by the "sham squire," the pet scoundrel of Dublin castle.

The *Press* was then the only popular paper in Dublin absolutely free from state control.

Lecky entirely ignores the statement that the informer, Wheatley, subsequently acknowledged his perjury—a further and most important proof of Orr's innocence.

If, after what the country has already seen and woefully experienced, ANY ENORMITY in the ruling system COULD excite popular astonishment, the flagitious persistency of *Faulkner's Journal*, to MURDER the fair fame of the martyred William Orr, after his life has been taken away —in a manner this country cannot forget—could not fail to astonish.

That a newspaper, bribed with the enormous peculation of THREE THOUSAND POUNDS a year, fleeced from a cheated country, should attempt to palliate the crimes—varnish the vices—and justify the strides of a profligate junto—is not wonderful. The pay-masters of *Faulkner's Journal*, the doers of that print, and the daily task it has formerly evinced of libelling the people of Ireland, and seeking to divide them by slanderously abusing one half, and stimulating against them the fanatical prejudices of the other, are things too notorious and too flagrant to escape public cognizance, and too detestable to meet public credit or public confidence.

On the villainous attack of that *Journal* upon the posthumous fame of the devoted victim ORR, let the last dying declaration of that virtuous man, as published in our last, flash refutation and damning contempt. Let those who would now endeavour to mitigate the pangs of conscience, by stabbing the character after they have destroyed the life of a virtuous citizen—read THAT declaration, and deprecate it if they will, the vengeance of Heaven due to their crimes. But neither the CROCODILE TEARS of a Yelverton, nor the corrupt panegyric or flagitious misprisons of a prostitute newspaper, will blot out the sin, or out-plead before " Heaven's chancery," the cries of the widow and the orphans.

The character of baron YELVERTON is lugged in amongst the justifications of WILLIAM ORR's sentence and catastrophe. Baron YELVERTON, in passing the sentence immediately after the conviction, merely complied with the form of the act of parliament. But what is to contravene the impeachment of a part of the very jury on their own verdict or what is to stand against the remorseful declaration of the principal witness against his own testimony ? Neither the jury, whose names we have given, nor the witness, who, like another Judas, remorsefully confest his own guilt, have come forward to support the assertions of *Faulkner's Journal*.

Against the probability of WILLIAM ORR's guilt, on the charge to which he had fallen a victim, stood his own character and conduct in every relative duty of life—as a citizen, as a son, as a husband, as a father, as a neighbour, as a friend, universally beloved and respected in his native country. He was a man, too, of sound understanding and discernment : and that SUCH a man, whatever might have been his political principles, after having seen so many lives forfeited to MILITARY EXECUTION and MILITARY EVIDENCE, would have been so foolishly unguarded as to tamper with the "REFINED LOYALTY" and " NICE HONOUR " of a "COMMON SOLDIER," is a circumstance not easy of credit with any rational being.

But it is not wonderful that the eminent respectability of WILLIAM ORR's character should render him the more eligible as a victim to that junto, with whom liberality of sentiment is a prescribed crime, and love of country the blackest treason.

How far these publications justify the first insertion in the *Belfast News-Letter* that William Orr had taken "THAT PUBLIC METHOD" (viz., an advertisement in that newspaper) to acknowledge his guilt and the justness of his sentence, let the public judge.

How far the conversation with the high sheriff and the rev. William Bristow, who interrupted him during his meditations over a religious book in his prison, in which they took so elaborate a part, whilst he only replied in a few cold and civil words, evidently calculated to cut short the intrusion ; how far this conversation justifies the malignant aspersions with which certain other newspapers have teemed, the reporter will not take upon himself to say. He wishes to confine himself to the chastest narrative of the facts, and to do justice equally to the living and the dead.

Two things are now certain, that William Orr never did sign a confession of his guilt, though urged and entreated so to do, in order to save his life ; and also that the high sheriff and William

WILLIAM BRISTOW,
VICAR AND SOVEREIGN OF BELFAST.

Bristow both refused to sign the memorial in his favour, which caused the refusal of many other gentlemen. They promised, it is true, to write privately to government the cause of their refusal, and it was hoped that they would have written in the same spirit of christian kindness which led them first to his prison to enquire WHETHER HE HAD EVERY COMFORTABLE ACCOMMODATION CONSISTENT WITH HIS UNHAPPY SITUATION, on that day when the election of a burgess accidentally called them to the town of Carrickfergus. Much was with reason expected from the humane representation of these gentlemen, both persons of consideration in the eyes of government, one of them high sheriff of the county, a gentleman of titled family, and a collector of his majesty's customs, the other a clergyman highly beneficed in the church, vicar-general of the diocese of Down and Connor, and lately appointed a chaplain to his excellency the lord lieutenant, a man of abilities, undoubtedly, whose services to government had been the cause of dispensing with his attendance at the court. On the other hand, the family of the prisoner, the private character of himself and his brother, were strong grounds for such powerful advocates to urge, when warmed with that sentiment of benevolence which first led them to his gaol.

Notwithstanding the extraordinary circumstances which occurred in the case of William Orr, to arrest the arm of the law, and rescue the life of a much-esteemed man from what has the appearance of a most flagitious conspiracy, he suffered at Carrickfergus.

Since such has been the inadvertable fate of William Orr—since such has been the inexorable determination of those who hold the sword of justice in Ireland, what has become of that most sacred principle of coronary discretion, that brightest gem in the royal diadem--the sacred and awful duty of executing justice with mercy, that revered and invaluable axiom, so long the boast of our jurisprudence—"that it were better AN HUNDRED GUILTY PERSONS should escape punishment, than ONE INNOCENT MAN should suffer"—or what shall we say of a power so concupiscent of victims, that not even the repentant declaration of abused and prejudiced jurors, not even the remorseful acknowledgements of a perjured witness to the falsehood of HIS OWN testimony, on which the verdict of William Orr reverted—cannot soothe to temperance, to mercy.

From the tyranny and prosecution of proud and unfeeling aristocracy—from military outrage, and magisterial oppression, the Irish subject still consoled himself, in the hope of an asylum under the sacred privilege of trial by jury, and looked for a sanctuary against prejudice and malevolence, even then in the benign and dispassionate exercise of royal clemency ; but after the lamentable fate of William Orr, who will rest on such hopes? Venerated shade of the immortal Camden, can such baleful fruits grow under the auspices of thine house, from that constitution and these laws which you have so ably taught us to revere.

The fate of the late William Orr has achieved (to the utter discomfiture of that ruthless system of disunion that had sought to arm the different religious sects against each other, and on the ruins of the altar and the church to erect the standard of despotism), and what perhaps no other human event could have so soon and effectually accomplished, the extinguishment of all religious disagreements, and the consolidation of rival affections. His dying declaration has convinced the catholics of a truth so much pains had been used to stifle, that he died in their cause, and for promotion of UNITED interests.

Madden says "lord Camden was deaf to all the representations made to him. All the waters of the ocean will not wash away the stain his obduracy on this occasion has left on his character. Better fifty thousand times for his fame, it were, if he had never seen Ireland. The fate of Orr lies heavy on the memory of lord Camden."

Major-general Napier states that viceroy Camden was a man of callous indifference to the feelings of others. Lady Louisa Connolly pleaded on her knees with him for permission to visit her dying nephew, lord Edward Fitzgerald, and he spurned her every request with almost unknown cruelty, drawing from her indignant breast the words, "I, who never before kneeled to aught but my God, grovelled at that man's feet in vain."

The following references from the *Press* relate to the conduct of the military in attacking and wrecking the printing houses in Belfast which had issued popular literature :—

On Friday, 27th October, colonel Barber called at a shop in Belfast, and in general Lake's name informed the owner that he understood that it was intended to publish a pamphlet respecting William Orr's trial, to inflame the minds of the lower order of the people, and that the wrecking of Mathew Smith's house might be an example of what should be done wherever it was found.

EXTRACT OF A LETTER FROM BELFAST.

On Monday last, an intimation having been given to some of the family of Mathew Smith, of this town, printer, that the military had meditated an attack upon his house and property, in consequence of his having several printed copies of the late William Orr's dying declaration in his possession, mrs. Smith waited upon general Lake and represented her fears, which the general listened to, and might (it may be presumed) in consequence, have timely prevented any mischief; but we are sorry to state, this application was fruitless, as in some time after a large party of the Monaghan militia, in the most outrageous manner, forcibly broke into Mathew Smith's house, and destroyed the furniture and printing materials, broke all the windows and doors, and have threatened the like destruction to every house where they can discover any of those papers to be. This is a new instance of that " VIGOUR BEYOND THE LAW," under which the liberty of a subject, the liberty of the press, the trial by jury, the right of popular assembly, and political discussion, the privilege of appeal to parliament, and petition to the throne for the redress of wrongs, have been annihilated to HELOTS of ERIN."

The general subsequently said to miss Rabb, a sister of mrs. Smith, that he intended to have interposed, but that he was prevented by an unfortunate visit from a methodist preacher, whose tediousness had occasioned the delay. Mathew Smith was a nephew of Samuel Neilson, and his wife was a daughter of John Rabb, printer of the *Northern Star*.

The recent outrage of the Monaghan militia upon the house and property of Mathew Smith, for no other crime than having in his POSSESSION a few copies of the dying declaration of William Orr, is a TOLERABLE specimen of what the people have to expect. The packing of juries, the subornation of witnesses, civil and military, and the solemn mockery of state trials, have by no means produced a proportion of victims adequate to the odium they have brought on their promoters, or the expense of near HALF-A-MILLION for proclamation prosecutions, secret service and other contingencies which it has cost the country, therefore the rulers of the ROAST have determined to economise and appeal to the sword, the musquet, the bayonet or the firebrand, as the most cheap and expeditious instruments of vengeance. It is the advise of an honest and humane CROWN lawyer. Jack Toler has counselled that no more prisoners be taken—PROBATUM EST : and therefore away with hideous forms, " Cry havoc, and let slip the dogs of war."

Jack Toler was the solicitor-general, afterwards lord Norbury, the hanging judge.

No man of the period sacrificed more for his principles than William Sampson, editor of the *Northern Star*. He was one of the counsel who defended William Orr prior to his own imprisonment and exile. To his pen and exertions we are entitled for the published trials of the *Northern Star*, and also of William Orr. The persecutions to which he was subjected are almost beyond parallel in the treatment of a political prisoner by any European nation. Sampson was the son of a clergyman of the established church, born in Derry, cultured and educated beyond the usual standard of that age. In the United States he rose to eminence at the bar, earning the affection and regard of his fellow-citizens. In 1831 he was entertained to a public banquet in Philadelphia, and on that occasion he took the opportunity as favourable for a review of some of the incidents in the trial of William Orr. He had been a personal friend of the victim as well as the counsel at his trial.

WILLIAM SAMPSON,
EDITOR OF THE NORTHERN STAR, ONE OF THE COUNSEL
WHO DEFENDED WILLIAM ORR.
(from a portrait at Ardrigh)

The following are the words he uttered :—

"Divide and conquer is the tyrant's maxim—Unite and conquer is the patriot's creed. He who takes this great principle for his leading star, and follows its guidance through storm and peril, will have done his duty, and, however adverse his destiny, his course has been the true one. If he has pursued it undauntedly and faithfully he may suffer shipwreck of his fortune or of his life, but never of his conscience or his honour. Such was that brave and honest man, who without pretensions to splendid genius or to mighty talents, and of that middle station where virtue is most apt to fix its habitation, and with whose honest name I am most proud to be identified—such was WILLIAM ORR. He was no boastful orator—no aspiring leader. His love was for his country and his sole ambition for its deliverance. You, who have never seen him as I have, may figure to yourselves a plain and honest countryman, but one upon whose front nature had stamped the virtues that dwelt within his breast. And, though it matters not what are the outward lineaments of him whose soul is pure and courage noble, yet, let me say, he was one in whose manly countenance, fine stature, and fair proportions was written MAN; and let me tell you now for what he died.

"Amongst the bloody acts of a ferocious parliament—scourges and traitors to their country, minions and sycophants of a foreign and a hostile government—there was one to which they gave the too just title of the insurrection act. In this there was a clause which made it felony of death to take unlawful oaths. To one not versed in Irish history it might appear that this enactment was to punish the exterminating oaths of those called peep-o'-day boys, afterwards orangemen. But no; these were encouraged, rewarded, and indemnified. It was at the great principle of union that they aimed, for that they knew would lead to liberty. Hear, then, the obligation for which this patriot was condemned by drunken jurors, perjured witnesses, and a judge who shed vain tears of contrition and compunction in passing the horrible sentence of death upon him. This it was—

"'In the presence of God, I do voluntarily declare that I will persevere in endeavouring to form a brotherhood of affection amongst Irishmen of every religious persuasion, and that I will also persevere in my endeavours to obtain an equal, full, and adequate representation of all the people of Ireland.'

"You have not heard it all. The conscience-stricken jury who found him guilty recommended him to mercy. Some of them came forward and, in open court, made solemn oath that liquor had been introduced into the room where they had retired to deliberate upon the verdict, and the result had been almost general intoxication; that one of the body had terrified them with denunciations of vengeance for their disloyalty; that still these fearful menaces against their persons and their dwellings would not have been sufficient to seduce them to so criminal an act, but the effects of the liquor they had taken and the deluding assertion that the life of William Orr was in no danger; that in their minds the case was doubtful, and that they had so stated it in giving their verdict.

"Stay yet a little, there is yet more to follow. The principal witness made a solemn oath that he felt great compunction for his crimes committed against Orr, and many others, and that what he swore against William Orr was false. A respite of his execution was granted, and much interest was made, for he was much beloved. Was it through mercy that this was granted? It was not, nor for the sake of justice. It was that two murders might be committed—the one upon his person, the other upon his good name. It was published in newspapers that he had confessed his guilt. They went into his cell and found him in the act of prayer. Mercy was offered upon the sole condition that he would acknowlege himself to be a guilty man. His fortitude was assailed through the affections of a brother, and the tears and prayers and lamentations of a beloved wife and five beloved children, by whatever could bind the affections of a fond husband and tender father to a sweet and happy home. Life was dear, for he was in the season of its best enjoyment; children and wife were dear, and friends were dear, but dear as all these were, his honour and his truth were dearer still.

"The story of his last moment, as I have heard it told by those who witnessed them, was thus:—' Upon the scaffold, nearest to him, and by his side, stood a Roman catholic domestic, faithful and attached to him. Manacled and pinioned, he directed them to take from his pocket the watch which he had worn till now that time had ceased for him, and his hours and minutes were no longer to be measures of his existence. "You, my friend, and I must part; our stations here on earth have been a little different, and our modes of worshipping the Almighty Being that we both adore. Before His presence we shall stand both equal; farewell, remember Orr.'"

" Here the scene closes—here let the curtain fall. I will not lead you through the tragic acts that followed on this murder, too hideous to be told—too foul to have a name. Let this serve as the epitome of Ireland's history; a government that ruled by crime and cruelty; a government that whilst it dealt death and exile, and torture and ruin to such men as this, allied itself with all that was corrupt and vile. And if I have any title to your favour, it is not from genius or talents which your partiality would impute to me, but that I have been, in my opposition to this misrule, sincere and resolute. And still may you remember me, when you remember Orr. And whilst I live I shall be grateful to you.

" I might perhaps have risen to higher fortunes, and had I stooped as low as others did, I might have worn a coronet, and left in dying, to my posterity, a high and sounding title to hereditary—infamy. With even less of talents or of genius than the little I possess, many have been so distinguished. And I think this is no mighty boast. The strange, iniquitous, relentless, mysterious persecutions that I have been honoured with, are proof that I was not held of small account, but the reward I have in the esteem and approbation of my country and honoured countrymen, and that of my country's friends, and the transmission of an honest name, is dearer far to me than baubles, that are now fallen full cheap in all discerning eyes—that even when earned by merit, serve but to counteract the great scheme of natural equality and right—and which by lifting up the few degrade the many, and which, when earned by patricidal treachery, are but objects of loathing, contempt and scorn, and so should remain, and so descend from generation to generation."

Of all the publications which appeared after the execution of William Orr the following letter of Marcus, which appeared in the *Press* of 26th October, was the most trenchant and galling to the government. The *Press* succeeded the *Northern Star*, of Belfast, the organ of the united Irishmen, which had been suppressed, and it in turn was put down by military force. The writer, Marcus, was an Englishman named Deane Swift, a descendant of Godwin Swift, uncle of the great dean.

TO HIS EXCELLENCY THE LORD LIEUTENANT.

MY LORD,—I address your excellency on a subject as awful and interesting as any that hath engaged the feelings of this suffering country. The oppression of an individual leads to the oppression of every member in the state, as his death, however speciously palliated by forms, may lead to the death of the constitution. Your lordship already anticipates me, and your conscience has told you that I allude to the circumstance of William Orr, whose case every man has now made his own by discovering the principle on which William Pitt sent you to EXECUTE his orders in Ireland.

By the death of William Orr the nation has pronounced one of the most sanguinary and savage acts that had disgraced the laws. In perjury, did you not hear, my lord, the verdict was given? Perjury, accompanied with terror, as terror has marked every step of your government. Vengeance and desolation were to fall on those who would not plunge themselves in blood. These were not strong enough. Against the express law of the land not only was drink introduced to the jury, but drunkenness itself, beastly and criminal drunkenness, was employed to procure the murder of a better man than any that now surrounds you. But well may juries think themselves justified in their drunken verdicts, if debauched and drunken judges, swilling spirits on the seat of justice itself, shall set the country so EXCELLENT an example.

Repentance, which is a slow virtue, hastened, however, to declare the innocence of the victim. The mischief which perjury had done truth now stept forward to repair; neither was she too late had humanity formed any part of your counsels. Stung with remorse, on the return of reason, part of his jury solemnly and soberly made oath that their verdict had been given under the unhappy influence of intimidation and drink, and in the most serious affidavit that ever was made, by acknowledging their crime, endeavoured to atone to God and to their country for the sin into which they had been seduced.

The informer, too, a man, it must be owned, not much famed for veracity, but stung with the like remorse, deposed that all he had formerly sworn was malicious and untrue, and that from compunction alone he was induced to make a full disclosure of his great and enormous guilt. In this confession the wicked man had no temptation to perjury; he was not to be paid for THAT; he had not in view, like another Judas, the "THIRTY PIECES OF SILVER"; if he was to receive his reward he knew he must not look for it in THIS world.

Those testimonies were followed by the solemn declaration of the dying man himself, and the approach of death is not a moment when men are given to deceive both themselves and the world. Good and religious men are not apt, by perjury on their death-bed, to close the gates of heaven against themselves, like those who have no hope. But, if these solemn declarations do not deserve regard, then is there no truth in justice; and, though the innocence of the accused had even remained doubtful, it was your duty, my lord—and you had no exemption from that duty—to have interposed your arm and saved him from the death that perjury, drunkenness, and reward had prepared for him.

Let not the nation be told that you are a passive instrument in the hands of others. If passive you be, then is your office a shadow indeed. If an active instrument, as you ought to be, you did not perform the duty which the laws required of you, you did not exercise the prerogative of mercy, that mercy which the constitution had entrusted to you for the safety of the subject, by guarding him from the oppression of wicked men. Innocent it appears he was. His blood has been shed, and the precedent indeed is awful.

Had Frazier and Ross [two yeomen] been found guilty of the murder committed on a harmless and industrious peasant—lay your hand to your heart, my lord, and answer without advisers—would you not have pardoned those ruffians? After the proof you have given of your mercy, I must suppose your clemency unbounded. Have no orangemen, convicted on the purest evidence, been at any time pardoned? Is not their oath of blood connived at? Was not that oath manufactured at the command of power and does not power itself discipline those brigands? But suppose the evidence of Wheatley had been true, what was the offence of William Orr? Not that he had taken an oath of blood and extermination—for then he had not suffered—but that he had taken an oath of charity and union, of humanity and of peace. He has suffered: shall we then be told, that YOUR government will conciliate public opinion, or that the people will not continue to look for a better?

Was the unhappy man respited but to torture him, to insult both justice and the nation, to carry persecution into the bosom of his wife and children? Is this the prerogative of mercy? What would your father have said unto you had he lived to witness this falling-off? "Son," he would have said, "I am a father; I have a DAUGHTER; I have known misfortune; the world has pitied me, and I am not ungrateful."

Let us explore the causes of this sanguinary destruction of the people. Is it that you are determined to revenge the regret expressed by them at the recall of your predecessor; and well knowing they will not shed tears at the departure of his successor, that you are resolved to make them weep during your stay? Yes, my lord, I repeat DURING YOUR STAY, for it may not be necessary that a royal yacht, manned and decorated for the purpose, should waft you from the shores of an angered and insulted country.

74

Another cause : Is it to be wondered that a successor of lord Fitzwilliam should sign the death-warrant of William Orr ? Pitt had learned that a merciful lord lieutenant was unsuited to a government of violence. It was no compliment to the native clemency of a CAMDEN, that he sent you into Ireland : and what has been our portion under the change, but massacre and rape, military murders, desolation and terror ?

Had you spared William Orr, you thought perhaps the numerous families of those to whom your administration had been devoted, might accuse you of partiality : and thus to prove your consistency, you are content to be suspected of wanting the only quality THIS country wishes you to exercise.

But, my lord, it will not do—though your guards and your soldiers, and your thousands, and your tens of thousands, should conduct innocence to death, it will not do—a voice has cried in the wilderness : and let the deserted streets of Carrickfergus proclaim to all the world, that good men will not be intimidated, and that they are yet more numerous than your soldiers.

We are not Domitian's people : we are not lopped at a blow : but it looks as if some fate had doomed us to be destroyed one by one, as the Persian tyrant ordered the hairs to be plucked from the tail of his beast. Beasts we have been, the vile carriers of the vilest burdens that the vilest masters could lay upon us. But the yoke is shaken : persecution has provoked to love, and UNITED Ireland against foreign despotism.

Feasting in your castle, in the midst of your myrmidons and bishops, you have little concerned yourself about the expelled and miserable cottager, whose dwelling, at the moment of your mirth, was in flames : his wife and daughter then under the violation of some commissioned ravager : his son agonizing on the bayonet, and his helpless infants crying in vain for mercy. These are lamentations that stain not the hour of carousal. Under intoxicated counsels the constitution has reeled to its centre : justice herself is not only blind-drunk, but deaf, like Festus, to " the words of soberness and truth."

My lord, the people of Ireland did hope that mercy would not have been denied to a most worthy and innocent man when they understood that one of the worst advisers and most imperious members of the cabinet had abandoned the kingdom. Had he been of your late counsels the odium might have been divided ; at present you have the best claim to it. Let, however, the awful execution of William Orr be a lesson to all unthinking juries, and let them cease to flatter themselves that the soberest recommendation of theirs and of the presiding judge can stop the course of carnage which sanguinary and, I do not fear to say, UNCONSTITUTIONAL LAWS have ordered to be loosed,; let them remember that, like Macbeth, the servants of the crown have waded so far in blood that they find it easier to go on than to go back.

I am, my lord,

Your excellency's humble servant,

MARCUS.

The publication of this letter soon brought about the prosecution of Peter Finnerty, the nominal proprietor of the *Press*. The real owner was Arthur O'Connor, nephew of lord Longueville.

At this trial the clerk of the crown read the arraignment of the traverser, an indictment for publishing in the *Press* of the 26th October, 1797, a false and scandalous libel, tending to bring into disrepute and scandal a verdict, etc., passed on William Orr, and charging his excellency with incapacity, cruelty, etc., in the administration of justice, particularly for not extending the mercy of the crown to the said William Orr after his conviction.

The indictment set out the greater part of the letter signed MARCUS in the *Press* of the 20th October.

The preposterousness of the prosecution is now apparent, "tending to bring into disrepute and scandal a verdict passed on William Orr"—a "verdict," by all that is just, an outrage, if you will, a wicked and scandalous outrage, with neither right nor justice in the smallest iota of it.

John Philpot Curran defended Peter Finnerty, making one of the most eloquent appeals ever heard in a court of justice.

The following is his description of the scenes which attended and followed the trial of William Orr :—

" Let me beg of you for a moment to suppose that any one of you had been the writer of this strong and severe animadversion upon the lord lieutenant, and that you had been the witness of that lamentable and never to be forgotten catastrophe ; let me suppose that you had known the charge upon which William Orr was apprehended —the charge of abjuring that bigotry which had torn and disgraced his country, of pledging himself to restore the people to their place in the constitution, and of binding himself never to be the betrayer of his fellow-labourers in that enterprise ; that you had seen him upon that charge torn from his industry and confined in gaol ; that through the slow and lingering progress of twelve tedious months you had seen him confined in a dungeon, shut out from the common use of air and of his own limbs ; that day after day you had marked the unhappy captive, cheered by no sound but the cries of his family or the clanking of his chains ; that you had seen him at last brought to his trial ; that you had seen the vile and perjured informer deposing against his life ; that you had seen the drunken and worn-out and terrified jury give in a verdict of death ; that you had seen the same jury, when their returning sobriety had brought back their reason, prostrate themselves before the humanity of the bench and pray that the mercy of the crown might save their characters from the reproach of an involuntary crime, their consciences from the torture of eternal self-condemnation, and their souls from the indelible stain of innocent blood. Let me suppose that you had seen the respite given, and the contrite and honest recommendation transmitted to that seat where mercy was presumed to dwell ; that new and before unheard of crimes are discovered against the informer ; that the royal mercy seems to relent ; that a new respite is sent to the prisoner ; that time is taken to see " whether mercy could be extended or not ; " that after that period of lingering deliberation had passed a third respite is transmitted ; that the unhappy captive himself feels the cheering hope of being restored to a family that he had adored, to a character that he had never stained, and to a country that he had ever loved ; that you had seen his wife and his children upon their knees giving those tears to gratitude which their locked and frozen hearts had refused to anguish and despair, and imploring the blessings of eternal Providence upon his head who had graciously spared the father and restored him to his children :—

> " Alas,
> Nor wife nor children more shall he behold,
> Nor friends, nor sacred home."

" Often did the weary dove return to the window of his little ark ; but the olive leaf was to him no sign that the waters had subsided. No seraph mercy unbars his dungeon, and leads him forth to light and life ; but the minister of death hurries him to the scene of suffering and of shame, where, unmoved by the hostile array of artillery and armed men collected together to secure, or to insult, or to disturb him, he dies with a solemn declaration of his innocence, and utters his last breath in a prayer for the liberty of his country."

This speech was one of Curran's masterpieces, and that is saying much of one of the most eloquent Irishmen that ever lived. The whole of it is well worth perusal. Were there no other memorial of William Orr, this speech alone would ever preserve his memory.

THE GRAVE OF WILLIAM ORR IN TEMPLEPATRICK.
(*from a photo*)

STREET BALLAD.

In October 'ninety-seven—
May his soul find rest in heaven—
William Orr to execution was led on
The jury, drunk, agreed
That Irish was his creed;
For perjury and threats drove them on, boys, on,
Here's the memory of the martyr that is gone.

77

WILLIAM ORR
(from a sketch by E. A. Morrow).

WAKE OF WILLIAM ORR.

BY WILLIAM DRENNAN.

Here our worthy brother lies;
Wake not HIM with women's cries;
Mourn the way that manhood ought;
Sit in silent trance of thought.

Write his merits on your mind;
Morals pure and manners kind;
On his head, as on a hill,
Virtue placed her citadel.

Why cut off in palmy youth?
Truth he spoke, and acted truth.
"Countrymen, UNITE!" he cried,
And died, for what his Saviour died!

God of peace, and God of love,
Let it not thy vengeance move,
Let it not thy lightnings draw;
A nation guillotined by law.

Hapless nation, rent and torn,
Early wert thou taught to mourn!
Warfare of six hundred years,
Epochs marked by blood and tears.

Hunted thro' thy native grounds,
A flung REWARD to human hounds;
Each one pulled and tore his share,
Emblem of thy deep despair.

Hapless nation—hapless land,
Heap of uncementing sand;
Crumbled by a foreign weight;
And by worse, domestic hate.

God of mercy, God of peace,
Make the mad confusion cease;
O'er the mental chaos move,
Through it speak the light of love.

Monstrous and unhappy sight,
Brother's blood will not unite;
Holy oil and holy water,
Mix, and fill the earth with slaughter.

Who is she with aspect wild?
The widowed mother with her child,
Child new stirring in the womb,
Husband waiting for the tomb.

Angel of this sacred place
Calm her soul and whisper, peace,
Cord, nor axe, nor guillotine
Make the sentence—not the sin.

Here we watch our brother's sleep,
Watch with us, but do not weep;
Watch with us through dead of night,
But expect the morning light.

Conquer fortune—persevere—
Lo! it breaks—the morning clear!
The cheerful COCK awakes the skies,
The day is come—arise, arise!

"FEMINIS LUGERE HONESTUM EST,
VIRIS ME MINISSE."

Ballymore, October, 1797.

The following is a list of the authorities which have been consulted, as well as those noted in the text :—

United Irishmen, 1, 2, 3, and 4th Series.   By R. R. Madden.
Secret Service under Pitt.   W. J. Fitz-Patrick.
The Sham Squire.   do.
Ireland before the Union.   do.
The Viceroy's Postbag.   Michael MacDonagh.
History of Ireland in the Eighteenth Century.   By W. E. H. Lecky.
Hardwicke MSS.
Lives and Trials.   Thomas MacNevin.
Memories of '98.   W. S. Smith.
Trial of William Orr.   Dublin, 1797.
Report from the Secret Committee.   Dublin, 1798.

The illustrations have been made from photos taken by the writer, and from drawings made by Joseph W. Carey and John Vinycomb under the writer's guidance, and from pictures in his possession.   The small type in the text indicates lengthened quotations.   The pikes depicted on the cover are accurately drawn from the collection at Ardrigh.

ERRATA :—The date " 18th October," in title to picture, page 52, should be " 15th."

WILLIAM ORR'S
Coleraines.

OLD LINEN SEAL OF THE ORRS
(in possession of Robert May).

Price 1/= (Net) EACH PART.

THE NORTHERN LEADERS OF '98.

By FRANCIS JOSEPH BIGGER, M.R.I.A.

(Editor of the " Ulster Journal of Archæology,"

ARDRIGH, BELFAST.

𝔉ully 𝔦llustrateð.

Part 1. – WILLIAM ORR.

The other Parts will include—

Henry Monro, Henry Joy M'Cracken, James Hope, Samuel Neilson and Thomas Russell.

———

The printing will be done in Ireland, on Irish paper, and the illustrations made there.

MAUNSELL & CO., Publishers, Dublin.

TO BE HAD FROM ALL BOOKSELLERS.

A very limited edition, to include all the parts, bound in Irish linen, can be had from the writer at **10/-** net.